The Desktop Publishing Companion

by

Graham Jones

SIGMA PRESS

First published in 1987 by

Sigma Press
98a Water Lane, Wilmslow, SK9 5BB, England.

ISBN 1 85058 078 2

British Library Cataloguing in Publication Data

Jones, Graham
The desktop publishing companion.
  1. Printing --- Data processing
  2. Publishers and publishing --- Data
processing
  I. Title
  070.5'028'516   Z249.3

Distributed by

John Wiley & Sons Ltd., Baffins Lane, Chichester, West Sussex, England.

Printed in Great Britain by J. W. Arrowsmith Ltd., Bristol

CONTENTS

Acknowledgments 4

Trade Marks 5

How this book was originated 7

Author's introduction 9

Chapter 1: Desktop Publishing. The Possibilities and Impossibilities 11

Chapter 2: Desktop Publishing Technology 21

Chapter 3: Publishing Basics 33

Chapter 4: Organising for Desktop Publishing 57

Chapter 5: Planning for Desktop Publishing 79

Chapter 6: Starting Desktop Publishing 107

Chapter 7: Beyond Desktop Publishing 127

Chapter 8: Desktop Publishing in Use 141

Chapter 9: Desktop Publishing Help 147

Bibliography 171

Glossary 175

Appendix 187

Index 199

Acknowledgments

I would like to thank the following people for the information and assistance they kindly provided during the compilation of this book:

Karen Alldred, Gestetner; Marc Balhetchet, Digital Technology; Graham Beech, Sigma Press; Karen Bernays, Inprint; Pat Bitten, Mirrorsoft; Henry Budgett, Desktop Publishing Company; Gail Capener, Apricot Computer PLC; Rod Clark, QED Technology; Andrew Clunies-Ross, Talbot Computers Ltd; Pat Coupland, CP&I Computer Services; Norman Evans, Creative Marketing Network, Toronto; Ian Fraser, IBM PC User Group; Mike Glover, Icon Technology; Derek Gray, Aldus UK; Elaine Griffiths, Heyden and Son; Graham Hallett, CCA Micro Rentals; David Hewson, Mandarin Publishing; Andrew James, Rank Xerox; David Jones, Apple Computers UK; Elliot Kahan, Heyden and Son; Bill Laws, Burson Marsteller; John Lewis, Mac User Group; Alisdair MacDonald, CCA Micro Rentals; Jim Maloney, Linotype Ltd; Joe Osiel, Print Three; Rothwell Data Systems; Bill Sadler, Heyden and Son; Tony Sanders, Rank Xerox; Scientext Ltd; Text 100; Andrew Tribute, Seybold Publishing; Friedman Wagner-Dobler, Cognita Software Ltd; Celia Woodward, Electronic Printing Systems; and Stefan Young, Mac Europe.

I would also like to thank all of the people who buy publications produced by my own desktop publishing system. Without them I would never have been in a position to write this book.

Graham Jones
Surrey, 1987

Trade Marks

The following is a list of trade marks and registered trade marks mentioned within this book. The owners of the trade marks and registered trade marks are in brackets after each one.

Acta (Symmetry Corporation) Advent (Advent Data Products) Agfa (Agfa Gevaert) Amstrad (Amstrad PLC) Apple ® (Apple Computer Inc) Apricot® (Apricot Computers PLC) Atari (Atari Corporation) AutoCAD® (Autodesk) ITC Avant Garde® (International Typeface Corporation) Clue (Clue Computing Company) Comic Works (Mindscape Inc) Cricket Graph (Cricket Software) Data Products® (Data Products Corporation) dBase III (Ashton Tate) DDL (Imagen) DEC® (Digital Equipment Corporation) Deskset (G.O Graphics) Diablo (Xerox Corporation) Dialtext® (Talbot Computers) Documentor (Xerox Corporation) Epson (Epson America Inc) Ethos (QED Technology Ltd) FDP (Digital Technology Ltd) Filevision (Telos Software Products) Fleet Street Publisher (Mirrorsoft) Fleet Street Editor (Mirrorsoft) Fontasy (Prosoft) Fontographer (Altsys Corporation) Front Page (Studio Software) FullPaint (Ann Arbor Softworks) ITC Garamond® (International Typeface Corporation) GEM (Digital Research Inc) Graphic Works (Mindscape Inc) Harvard Professional Publisher (Software Publishing Corporation) Helvetica® (Allied Corporation) HP (Hewlett Packard) IBM® (International Business Machines) ImageWriter (Apple Computers Inc) Interpress (Xerox Corporation) JetSetter (Electronic Printing Systems) JustText (Knowledge Engineering) Kyocera (Kyocera) Laser Jet® (Hewlett Packard) Laser Jet Plus ®(Hewlett Packard) Laser Master (Xitan) Laser Tools (Knowledge Engineering) Laser Type V Plus (Whizz Computing Company Inc) LaserWriter (Apple Computer Inc) LaserWriter Plus (Apple Computer Inc) Letraset® (Esselte Letraset Ltd) Linotronic 100, Linotronic 300 (Allied Corporation) Lotus 123® (Lotus Development Corporation) Mac-Hy-phen (MicroCosmos) MacAuthor (Icon Technology) MacBottom (Personal Computer Peripherals Corporation) MacDraft (Innovative Data Designs) MacDraw (Apple Computer Inc) Macintosh (licensed to Apple Computer Inc. by McIntosh Laboratories Inc.) MacPaint (Apple Computer Inc) MacPublisher II (MicroCosmos) MacVision (Koala Technologies Corporation) MacWrite (Apple Computer Inc) MegaScreen (MicroGraphic Images Corporation) Microsoft® (Microsoft Corporation) Microsoft Word (Microsoft Corporation) Microsoft Windows (Microsoft Corporation) MS-DOS (Microsoft Corporation) MultiMate (MultiMate International) NewsWriter (Cognita Software Ltd) Omnis 3 Plus (Blyth Software Ltd) PageMaker® (Aldus Corporation) Palatino® (Allied Corporation) PC-AT (International Business Machines) PC-DOS® (International Business Machines) PC-XT (International Business Machines) PC Paint (Mouse Systems Corporation) PosterMaker (Strider Software) PostScript (Adobe Systems Inc) Protex (Scientex Ltd) Protégé (QED Technology Ltd) PTW (Itek Graphix) Ragtime (Orange Micro) Ready Set Go 3 (Manhattan Graphics Corporation) Samna Word 4 (Samna Corporation) SoftQuad (Soft Quad) ITC Souvenir® (International Typeface Corporation) Spectrum 128 (Amstrad PLC) Symphony (Lotus Development Corporation) TeX (American Mathematical Society) The Office Publisher (Laser Friendly) Thunderscan (Thunderware Inc) Times (Allied Corporation) Unix (AT&T) Ventura Publisher (Ventura Software Inc) Windows Paint and Draw (Microsoft Corporation) Word Perfect (SSI Software) Wordstar® (MicroPro International Corporation) Writer's Workshop (Futuresoft System Design) Xenix (Microsoft Corporation) Xerox (Xerox Corporation) Xtraset (Typecraft (UK) Ltd)

How this book was originated

This book was written using MacAuthor on an Apple Macintosh Plus computer linked to a MacBottom hard disk. The page designs included in the book as examples were prepared using PageMaker, and the other graphics were produced using MacDraw and MacPaint. The whole book was originally outlined using Acta. The master pages were printed out on an Apple LaserWriter Plus.

The typeface used is New Century Schoolbook, which is a Public Domain typeface. Other typefaces used in this book are Times, Avante Garde, Palatino and Helvetica. Trade mark acknowledgment is given on page 3.

Author's Introduction

This book is not about computers but about publishing. Computers are merely tools with which we can produce publications. Sadly, the publicity surrounding desktop publishing as a concept appears to have made some people believe that there are programs on the market which will convert them into publishers. These people fail to remember that no wordprocessing program has converted an illiterate into a Shakespeare. So no desktop publishing program is likely to convert an individual into a Harold Evans. Hopefully though, this book will alert those convinced and those interested in the benefits of desktop publishing, to the incredible similarities between desktop publishing and traditional publishing. The new wave of desktop publishers can learn a lot from the well established traditional publishing industry. I hope that this book will point the way and will help desktop publishers to produce professional results. Sadly, many desktop publishers have hoped that the software will convert them into instant publishing designers, and consequently the results have sometimes been quite poor. The following are selected quotes from a software advertisement which aptly sum up the whole problem.

'When the rhetoric is swept away along with all the deflated publicity balloons and desktop publishing is examined on the reasonable basis of what has actually been achieved, it's a pound to a prick of printer's ink you'll agree there's not a lot to show.

Professional designers have been staying away in their droves. And without their skills it's not surprising that results are mostly disappointing. Good design does not appear as an item on a pull-down menu after all. It's not something you get from a quick course. You can't invoke it as a Desk Accessory.

On the contrary, good design results from flair, talent, inspiration, and a lot of training. That's why artists, graphic designers and typographers serve long apprenticeships at school.'

Quotes taken from a January 1987 advertisement for the Apple Macintosh desktop publishing program 'JustText'. Quotes reproduced by permission of MacEurope with grateful thanks.

Chapter 1

Desktop Publishing. The Possibilities and Impossibilities

Since the beginning of 1986 the words 'Desktop Publishing' have taken a variety of meanings. To some desktop publishing is the ability to print out attractive looking documents in a variety of typestyles using only a simple wordprocessor. To others it is the use of microcomputers to control powerful typesetting equipment. However, in reality neither of these definitions describes true desktop publishing.

Desktop publishing, as originally invented and as defined in this book, is the use of microcomputers to produce publications which previously required traditional publishing technology, or which would have required the old technology had the new publications been produced in the past. In other words, desktop publishing offers either a replacement for old technology in the publishing business, or because of the low price of the equipment enables the production of publications which would have been too costly to produce using the old technology.

Desktop publishing involves all of the aspects of production used in the traditional publishing industry. Desktop publishing is made up of writing, design, graphics and typography. Desktop publishing is not simply about the production of attractively presented wordprocessed material. It is much much more than that.

Desktop publishing allows an individual or an organisation to print copies of their own publication on the desktop, or to produce 'camera ready artwork' as the basis for traditional printing. Until the invention of desktop publishing the production of such artwork required a team of people to put it together. At the very least this would have been the originator of the work, a typesetter and a 'compositor' — the person who laid out the typeset copy on the page. Usually more people would be involved, thus increasing the likelihood of errors and the amount of time taken to perform the task. Now, with the use of desktop publishing technology, a page of a publication can be produced in hours, even minutes, rather than days.

The new technology produces the pages of any publication laid out as the originator wants them to appear without the need for a compositor. Typesetting can also be dispensed with, since the new technology produces near typeset quality pages, and can even be linked to high quality typesetting machines if necessary. The originator of the material can also have a much greater degree of control over the final product and can quickly and cheaply test a number of different designs, without the need to pay for comparatively expensive typesetters, to produce a variety of trial pages.

Desktop publishing makes a whole range of previously expensive options available to publishers, commercial organisations and individuals. We shall be exploring many of these possibilities later in this book.

However, in order to reap the benefits of the amazing leap forward which has brought us desktop publishing you will require at least a basic system. We shall be investigating the benefits and pitfalls of the major systems available in the next chapter. You will initially require a microcomputer which supports high screen resolution graphics, has a fairly large Random Access Memory (RAM) of at least 512 kilobytes, has at least two disk drives (although a hard disk is much easier to work with when running desktop publishing programs) and has good expansion ability. There are a number of additional items which many people involved in desktop publishing are now finding essential, such as image scanners which can convert pictures into on—screen graphics for placing in publications. As well as the computer you will also require a printer which can produce near typeset quality pages with a variety of typefaces. The only printers which fit the bill are called laser printers since they depend upon a fine laser beam to function.

As well as this basic hardware anyone involved in desktop publishing will require a minimum of software. This would be a wordprocessor, and a page layout program, and usually also an object oriented graphics program. Object oriented graphics programs are those which clearly define each element of a graphic, rather than assembling it from a collection of small units called 'pixels'. Because object oriented graphics define, for example the thickness of a line, and its position on a page, they can be reproduced accurately on a high resolution laser printer. However, graphics which are made up from pixels will reproduce less clearly.

Together with the basic hardware these programs would allow anyone to go ahead and produce publications on the kitchen table, without ever needing to go near a typesetting factory or a printer. That is why the new technology is designated 'desktop' publishing.

So what can you do with all of this technology once you have set it up? As already explained, you can use the new technology to produce any kind of publication which currently utilises the traditional publishing technology, or you can produce publications which would have been too expensive to produce using the old technology, but which can now be produced cheaply and quickly.

For example, many small groups and societies who would like to have a professional looking newsletter or magazine but are unable to afford the costs of design, typesetting and so on, can now use a member's computer to produce such a publication. Another use for desktop publishing might be the production of a *daily* staff newspaper for a big organisation, such as a high street bank. Using traditional publishing techniques such an exercise would be complicated and costly.

Desktop publishing can also be used by authors. This book was written on a desktop publishing system, and the master pages printed out on a laser printer, thus avoiding the need for costly and time consuming typesetting. These master pages were then passed on to the printer who was able to make up the finished copies of the book in the same way as he would have done if a typesetter had provided the 'camera ready' master pages.

Journalists too can use desktop publishing for much of their work. Indeed, Apple Computers, the company which first exploited desktop publishing, has a special deal whereby journalists can buy systems at considerable discounts. Freelance journalists have found this scheme particularly attractive. Buying a desktop publishing system enables a journalist to produce material and show it to clients in a form exactly as it might be published, thus allowing editors to get a much better idea of what the article would look like in print. In addition, many freelance journalists produce newsletters and so on for commercial clients. Desktop publishing technology allows these to be produced much more speedily and at a lower cost.

Because of the low production costs and, more importantly, the considerable time savings offered by desktop publishing systems, they can also be behind the production of new publications which would have been too costly to produce using the standard publishing techniques. Such publications might be very short–run books and manuals, or magazines and newsletters for a fairly small circulation. One example is the first ever commercial publication produced with a desktop publishing system. This is called *The Wordsmith* and is a magazine aimed at writers of all kinds who use computers in their work — whether or not they are desktop publishing systems! The magazine is produced six times each year and was the brainchild of Fleet Street journalist, David Hewson.

Within a year of publication *The Wordsmith* became one of the most important sources of information on computerisation and writing for many authors and journalists. Another new publication which is produced utilising desktop publishing is a monthly newsletter called *Desktop Publisher*.This provides the desktop publishing industry with up to the minute news and information on new products.

There are other outlets for desktop publishing as well as for authors, journalists and new publishers. An obvious one is in existing publishing houses. A desktop publishing system will enable magazine editors to test their ideas out, producing near typeset quality pages showing them layouts, graphics and so on. This will save time and the costs of typesetting. Consequently using a desktop publishing system in large publishing houses will lead to greater creativity and a wider range of design being put into practice. In other words, desktop publishing will provide editors with a creative tool which was not available until the beginning of 1986.

Despite the obvious use of desktop publishing in the world of books, magazines and newspapers there is a potential use for desktop publishing, which could well revolutionise many businesses. For desktop publishing systems will allow every kind of business, from the self–employed to giants like ICI or Boeing to produce all sorts of in–house and external publications which could not have been put together without expense and time. The use of desktop publishing in business is likely to be the largest single use of the new technology.

In–house newsletters and magazines will be possible. So too will training manuals, proposals and annual reports — all of which generally have to be farmed out to specialist agencies at extra costs and then have to be typeset, increasing both costs and production times. With desktop publishing technology these sorts of publications can all be put together in–house quickly.

In addition, the use of desktop publishing technology will also enable the preparation of much more attractive reports and other printed material which can include graphics thus increasing their appeal and readability. In fact desktop publishing could lie behind a major revolution in business communications contributing to a massive improvement in effectiveness and speed.

Marketing departments, for example, can now produce brochures, direct mail material and other sales aids quickly and easily, and can update them literally at the touch of a button or two, eliminating payments to third parties such as typesetters and motor cycle messengers. Public relations departments will be able to produce customer newsletters and magazines for potential customers. They will also be able to produce press materials, which project a much more 'professional' image, thus helping to enhance the company's reputation.

Company advertising departments can use desktop publishing systems to produce advertisements, or to test out ideas for advertisements. One desktop publishing system specially geared up for advertisers even does the scheduling for an advertising campaign, thus also helping with co–ordination.

A personnel department can use desktop publishing to produce staff newsletters and magazines. Many large organisations already have a staff newspaper, but because of the need to use outside typesetters these publications can take weeks to put together. Desktop publishing technology makes it possible to reduce the timescale, thus allowing more issues per year, increasing in–house communications and probably helping to make the staff feel 'at home' and 'wanted'.

As can be seen from these few examples, desktop publishing technology is behind a major revolution in communications, both in business and in the world of traditional publishing. Its two basic roles are to replace existing slow and costly methods of producing a publication, and to allow the production of publications which previously would have been too costly, or time consuming, to put together.

People who are involved in publishing already, and convert to desktop publishing technology, will find that by doing so they can achieve three main improvements. Firstly, after training, the operating costs of desktop publishing are far cheaper than those of traditional publishing. In most instances there is no longer a need for typesetting; there is no need to pay for motorcycle messengers or delivery services to shunt copy and typesetting around; and in many instances fewer staff are required to perform the whole operation. Even if capital costs are considered, these can be recovered remarkably quickly, and are less than one–third of the capital costs involved in purchasing even the most basic typesetting equipment.

The second advantage of desktop publishing is the increased flexibility it provides. For example, say an editor of a publication wants to change a headline from black type to white type on a black background. With traditional publishing techniques it would require the page being sent back to the typesetters, the work being performed and the changed page being returned to the editor. This will, at the very least, take some hours but in many instances may take a day or two. And when the editor sees the result it might not look good and will need changing back. Using desktop publishing techniques, however, the change from black type to white type takes no more than *ten seconds*. If the editor is not happy with the look of the change the material can be altered a number of times until it looks right.

Not only does this provide greater flexibility for editors and other producers of published material, but it also shows the third great improvement of desktop publishing over traditional techniques — increased speed.

Traditional publishing requires publishers to send material to typesetters, often many miles away, to be set in the chosen typestyle and positioned on the page according to a roughly drawn 'layout'. This page is then returned to the publisher, who has to check it for corrections and probably alter it in some way so that any excess material is cut, or gaps are filled. The material is then sent back to the typesetter who performs all of the corrections and returns the page to the publisher who will check that the corrections have been done properly. This all takes time, especially if the typesetter is so far away communication has to be performed by post!

Using desktop publishing systems means that all of this time wasting can be cut drastically. The screens of most of the computers show you exactly what will be printed meaning that you can check everything before you print — your first print—out can be your final attempt! In addition to this aspect of time saving, most of the page layout programs available are super efficient at saving time on things which extremely expensive typesetting systems are still incapable of performing. For example, if a picture has text which flows all the way around it moving the picture will mean that a traditional typesetter will have to reset the entire page in many instances, taking hours.

Some sophisticated desktop publishing programs can move the picture and re—work the text around it in just a few seconds. It is this sort of speed which makes desktop publishing so useful, so flexible and creative. You will hear computer dealers talk of the speed at which the programs are able to print off the material, though, and claim that some programs are slower than others. Whilst this may be true, the differences in printing speed between various programs are negligible in comparison to the difference between the slowest program and traditional methods of publishing. So don't be put off too much by computer dealers who tell you that the program you want has a slow printing speed! Compared to traditional publishing techniques all types of desktop publishing systems are remarkably fast.

However, despite all of these advantages of desktop publishing systems, there are some disadvantages.

The major disadvantage is the quality of the output of the laser printers. These printers work like photocopiers but instead of printing from an original document, as in copying, laser printers utilise a laser beam to provide the information about the printing areas of the page. This laser beam switches on and off rapidly as it passes over the printing drum — up to 300 times in every inch, in most cases.

Whenever the laser beam is switched on the drum becomes electrically charged and this becomes an area to which toner ink will be attracted. When paper is pressed against the printing drum the inked areas are transferred to the paper.Consequently it is possible to achieve 300 dots of printed toner ink in every inch. Most laser printers provide 300 dots per inch. So each square inch contains 90,000 dots. Some laser printers provide 400 dots per inch (160,000 per square inch) or 600 dots per inch (360,000 per square inch). However, even low cost typesetting machines provide something like 1,200 dots per inch (1,440,000 per square inch), whilst high quality machines provide 2,500 dots for every inch (6,250,000 per square inch). A top end typesetting machine like this has 70 dots for every one dot of basic laser printers.

Letters and graphics produced with 300 dots per inch have less clearly defined edges than those machines outputting at 1,200 or 2,500 dots per inch. The difference in quality for most purposes is not particularly important. The master pages for this book, for example, were printed on a 300 dots per inch laser printer. For high quality work involving lots of complicated graphics, and perhaps printed on glossy paper in full colour, a higher resolution may be needed.

For such publications, typesetting quality of at least 1,200 dots per inch is needed. This is not outside the scope of the programs which have made desktop publishing possible. These same programs can drive typesetting units and so pages made up using a desktop publishing system can be outputted on a typesetting machine, without the need for any extra work. However, this does extend the definition of 'desktop' publishing a little, since a typesetting machine is hardly desktop size, unlike laser printers. Such large machines are also around five to ten times the price of most laser printers. Desktop publishers, though, can use these machines since a number of typesetters and specialist bureaux offer the facilities for a small fee. This means that if, as a desktop publisher, you really are worried about quality you can produce actual typeset pages by using such services, though at somewhat greater cost and a longer timescale.

The other main problem with desktop publishing systems, and the one most frequently overlooked, is the fact that they all require an operator to be fairly well versed in publishing technique. Whilst the new technology replaces the cumbersome and time–consuming tasks of typesetting and composing it does not remove the need for writing ability, design and editing skills. From some of the examples of early desktop publications, you could be forgiven for thinking that the operators had bought the system in the hope that it would put a publication together for them! No system can do that — yet.

When using desktop publishing systems an operator still has to make all of the decisions about presentation, number of pages, size of pages, orientation, typefaces and type sizes, and so on. Hopefully, much of this book will guide you in to making the right sorts of choices for the work you are doing with your desktop publishing system.

One final disadvantage of desktop publishing systems is that they do not prepare people for the problems which all publishers suffer — marketing, sales and distribution. No matter how professional your publication may look, if you cannot get people to buy it (or accept it, if it is free) then your efforts will have been in vain. And if you can obtain a supply of readers, you are still faced with the problem of getting the publication to them — distribution.

Any desktop publisher, who ignores marketing and distribution, will do so at risk of having to sell off the system before too long, as it is not paying its way. Even in–house freely distributed reports and newsletters for companies need to be 'sold' to readers and properly distributed if they are to be read and have their desired effect. Later chapters will be looking at these problems in greater depth and will also hopefully provide some pointers as to effective methods.

The final disadvantage of desktop publishing systems for some people is price. As already mentioned a basic desktop publishing system requires a powerful computer with at least two disk drives and a high resolution screen as well as a laser printer and fairly complicated programs. The result is a cost of at least £5,000 ($7,500) for a very basic system and truly useable systems don't really come for less than £10,000 ($15,000) at 1987 prices. With various add–ons, a system can cost as much as £16,000 ($24,000) and compatible typesetting machines start at around £25,000 ($37,500). You could therefore spend as much as £41,000 ($61,500) on a top of the range desktop publishing system. However, a good, extremely capable system will cost about one quarter of this — £10,000 ($15,000). It is this price which puts many people off buying a system. Why should they lash out this amount of money, when they can use their £400 wordprocessor and send material in to a typesetter? Well, for many people this is a perfectly adequate option. However, for others the advantages of desktop publishing far outweigh the cost considerations.

There are also other costs to consider than the price of the system. Because most desktop publishing systems require their operators to have some basic idea about typography and design the cost of training also needs to be considered. There is also one additional cost to take into account, which not too many computer dealers will tell you about. This is the cost of creative time—wasting. Because of the flexibility of the majority of the systems it is possible to create virtually limitless designs and layouts for each and every page you put together. This ability means that it is very easy to use desktop publishing systems to try out a variety of page layouts and designs before you produce one which completely satisfies your artistic nature! This can be a waste of time. Many of the page layouts and designs you produce will be appropriate and attractive, and to look for possible alternatives may be futile. Keep an eye on the clock!

Altogether though, the possibilities of a desktop publishing system are immense, whereas the impossibilities are few and very easily overcome.

APRICOT DESKTOP PUBLISHING

Apricot's Desktop Publishing Systems are based on Apricot's XEN IBM compatible range of micros. Here the XEN-i, with 1 MB RAM and 20 MB Winchester disk, is pictured running Aldus PageMaker.

Chapter 2

Desktop Publishing Technology

The basic requirements for a desktop publishing system are a microcomputer with at least 512k of RAM and two disk drives, a laser printer and the appropriate software. However, there are a number of other considerations which need to be made before opting for a system which most suits your needs.

The Screen

Firstly, anyone dealing with any kind of publication likes to have a good idea of how the final item will appear in print. In traditional publishing this is achieved by the production of 'proofs' from the typesetter — photocopies of the typeset material. When using desktop publishing technology, however, the speed with which things can be done makes the production of proofs somewhat tiresome. Consequently desktop publishers require a screen display which shows them exactly what will be printed on each page. Most desktop publishing systems have true 'What You See Is What You Get' (WYSIWYG). The computer screen shows an accurate representation of the page layout, the typefaces and sizes, graphics and so on.

In order to achieve true WYSIWYG a desktop publishing system really requires a screen capable of high resolution graphics. This will enable the image on the screen to be an accurate drawing of each printed character.

Another factor is that for the screen to show true WYSIWYG it really needs to be a 'paper white' screen, showing black characters on a white background, just like printing on paper. Looking at bright green letters on a black background, as on some screens, does not give a true impression of what will be printed. Most people performing any kind of publication production will agree on the fact that as true a representation as possible of the final printed output is an important requirement, whichever kind of technology you use. So we now have two more requirements for our desktop publishing computer. It needs a high resolution graphics screen, and really ought to be paper white, showing lettering in black.

Sadly, there are very few computers which have this sort of sophistication. The Apple Macintosh, the brand leader in the world of desktop publishing, holding over 70 per cent of the market in 1986, has a high resolution paper white screen. However, the most popular computers, the IBM PC or compatibles, have a variety of screen colours. This means that if you already have such a computer you will need to adapt it prior to any desktop publishing work. Fortunately, most IBM type machines do have high resolution screens and the IBM PC itself has a higher resolution than the Apple Macintosh. However, since the Macintosh screen is only half the size of the IBM PC's screen the effect produced by the Macintosh is much crisper.

The resolution of the screen is important for desktop publishing work. It enables you to gain a much clearer impression of what will be printed. The higher the screen resolution, the more accurate the WYSIWYG. Like a laser printer a computer screen produces a number of dots per square inch. The larger the number of dots available per inch to construct each on—screen character, the more accurate the representation. This accuracy is really needed in desktop publishing, especially when using a combination of type sizes and when trying to ensure that everything lines up correctly. With true WYSIWYG this is possible. With no WYSIWYG, or a poor representation caused by a low resolution screen, such accuracy becomes difficult and a number of test pages are required to achieve the desired effect.

For people who have an IBM PC or a compatible the screen resolution problem is easily overcome by ensuring that additional hardware is available for the machine. This means that your chosen IBM compatible machine must have expansion slots available for the addition of extra printed circuit boards which allow the screen to perform graphic functions at high resolution. On a standard IBM PC, for example, you will be unable to see the *actual* type style in use for a given word, line, sentence or paragraph. You will be told what style is in use but you will not see what will be printed.

This is because the IBM PC does not support the graphics flexibility which is required to shape each individual character of a whole range of typefaces and sizes. To do that you need to expand the hardware. Fortunately the IBM PC and many compatibles have sufficient space in the computer itself to be able to take the additional printed circuit boards which will control the graphics of the screen. Some IBM compatibles do not have sufficient space for extra boards; expanding these computers into a true WYSIWYG machine can be virtually impossible, and therefore they will be of little help in desktop publishing use. Always check that the machine you buy has sufficient 'expansion slots' to be able to take on the extra printed circuit boards that you will require for desktop publishing graphics. Do not be misled into believing that since you will only be dealing with text you will not require a graphics expansion card. The text itself is a graphic, since each letter of each different typeface is drawn individually depending upon the size required. Your computer will not be able to perform this function without good graphics capability.

Memory

Another crucial requirement for a desktop publishing computer is a large Random Access Memory (RAM). This is the memory which contains the program you are working with and the information you are manipulating with that program.

In the main programs, which desktop publishers use, the page layout programs are complex and therefore very large. An average page layout program can take up as much as 300 kilobytes. Some are worth megabytes and are stored on a large number of disks. So when the program is loaded into the RAM of the computer you will need at least the size of the program, as well as more RAM on which to work. This is why you will require a computer with at least 512k of RAM to run the best desktop publishing programs effectively. To be really efficient though, you will need a computer with at least one megabyte of RAM, since this will allow you to manipulate larger documents with relative ease.

The size of the programs also brings about another requirement for the basic desktop publishing computer, two disk drives. For disk drives which are capable of coping with a large amount of data, such as the 800k drives of the Apple Macintosh Plus, you will be able to have the operating system and the program resident on one disk. The remaining disk drive will be useful for saving work as you go along. For disk drives which can only cope with a small amount of data, such as 5 $\frac{1}{4}$ inch drives handling only 300 kilobytes, a second drive is essential since the operating system will not fit onto the same disk as the program. Even with two disk drives there would need to be some disk swapping to enable material to be saved to a datadisk.

Anyone who tells you that you can perform desktop publishing with two floppy drives has probably never been seriously involved with desktop publishing at its best. A hard disk — which typically has 10 or 20 megabytes of storage — is vital since it saves endless disk swapping and is faster at retrieving information stored on it than a floppy disk drive. A hard disk will also be a useful place for storing standard page layouts and other items which are repeated on all of your publications, such as logos, special graphics and so on. If these were kept on a floppy disk you would need a large number of disk swaps in order to compile your publication, thus increasing the production time and providing a large amount of frustration for the operator!

Hard disk drives will contain a large amount of data and software, and are therefore very convenient to use. If an error occurs and there is damage to the disk the losses can be significant. Anyone with a hard disk should therefore ensure that they back up their work to floppies, or to a second hard disk, on a daily basis. It is important too to have a hard disk maintainance contract from a reputable dealer, or from the hard disk manufacturer. This will save considerable time and expense in the event of something going wrong with the disk. If a hard disk does break down, and you do not have a maintainance contract, you could wait some time before you are able to carry on working efficiently.

So there you have your basic desktop publishing computer. It is a machine which has at least 512k of RAM and preferably has one megabyte; it has a paper white screen with high resolution graphics capabilities; and it has at least two disk drives, though in reality a hard disk is more efficient. With these three basics you can operate a desktop publishing system. However, there is one other virtually essential item of hardware which makes desktop publishing more 'user friendly'. That item is a 'mouse'.

Mouse

A mouse is a pointer device attached to the computer, which allows an operator to point to items on the screen.

By using a mouse with a desktop publishing system you can point at an article, for example, and move it to a different place on the page.

Without a mouse you will often need to enter quite a lot of keyboard information to do this.

In fact, desktop publishing virtually depends upon what is known as a 'WIMP' environment. WIMP stands for Windows, Icons, Mouse and Pointers. A window is an area on the screen in which you can work. It is usually possible to have a number of windows open on the screen so that you can transfer work from one item to another. Or you can have important reference material present on the screen all of the time you are working on other documents, for example. Windows are a highly sophisticated method of split screening. The Apple Macintosh was designed around the concept of windows and consequently is ideally suited to desktop publishing. However, most IBM compatibles do not support windows without additional software, such as Microsoft Windows or the Digital Research Graphics Environment Manager (GEM).

Icons are images. Icon is the Greek word for image or likeness and in computing terms an icon is a small picture which represents a particular item. Consequently programs can be represented on-screen by one type of icon, whilst a saved document has another style of icon. When these icons are pointed at using the mouse, or some other kind of pointing device, the particular item can be launched and transferred into the RAM allowing work to be performed.

Without an icon and a mouse codes would have to be typed into the keyboard of the computer and, quite frequently, you would have to read a long list of items to find the one in which you were interested. With icons individual items are much more easily identifiable.

Because desktop publishing is essentially a creative task, learning 'computerspeak' is generally not something which most users would wish to do. Indeed, many of the potential users of desktop publishing, such as authors, journalists, advertising designers and public relations officers, may be put–off using computers for their creative work, since the widely held view of new technology is that you have to learn a lot of codes to get it to do what you want. With a WIMP environment you just point to what you want and let the computer sort it all out on your behalf. Consequently, a desktop publishing system which is supported by a WIMP style program enables the users to get on with the creative work, allowing the computerisation to deal with itself. Essentially, WIMPs are much more user–friendly than the traditional methods of using a computer.

Expansion

One final point about the computer you use for desktop publishing: it must be expandable. The requirements given above are really the basics needed to start off in desktop publishing proper. No doubt many people will tell you that they can produce newsletters easily with a Spectrum 128 and a dot–matrix printer.

Maybe they can, but it can hardly be described as professional desktop publishing, which is the main concern of this book. For applications of a high standard — and the standards are increasing every week — you will require the minimum described here. However, there are many additional items which are invaluable to desktop publishing, all of which you will probably want to add to your system at some stage. So make sure your computer is capable of being added to.

For example, you may wish your desktop publishing to be performed by a team of people. You will therefore require that the machine is workable in a network. This may only be possible with some additional hardware, so make sure it can be added. You might want to add pictures and drawings produced outside the computer. These will need scanning on a special image scanner before they can be recorded in the computer you are using. This machine will also need a linkage to your computer. Many desktop publishers find a modem invaluable in obtaining written material from correspondents around the country. A modem is a device which converts computer–based information into signals which can be transmitted down telephone lines. Modems also translate any material received by telephone so that it may be understood by the computer.In this way two computers, each linked to a modem, can communicate with each other over long distances using telephone connections. You might also want to add a large screen capable of showing full size pages in WYSIWYG form. All of these are options already open to desktop publishers, and no doubt many more will be added. But unless you want to run up the expense of having to purchase a new computer every year or so, make sure that the one you buy for desktop publishing is adaptable and expandable. If you are already using a computer for other work and would like to add desktop publishing to your system, you should first make sure that your computer has the necessary expansion potential — otherwise, you will have to think about changing your computer. For most people this will mean a suitable IBM PC or compatible, or the Apple Macintosh.

Laser Printers

Having chosen your computer, or adapted your current machine, you will then need to decide upon a suitable printer. As already explained, to be really effective you will need a laser printer for desktop publishing, rather than any other kind. Laser printers are much more than simple, effective machines for converting your work into hard copy. They are, in actual fact, powerful computers in their own right. Indeed, the laser printer manufactured by Apple Computers to go with the Apple Macintosh computer has one and a half megabytes of RAM — 50 per cent more than the top of the range one megabyte Macintosh Plus! Most other laser printers also have huge RAMs and are powerful computers in their own right.

The reason for this is relatively simple. When a computer tells a laser printer to produce a particular character, for example, a lot more information is passed down the line than a simple 'print the letter "G" in upper case bold'. Desktop publishing also describes the size, the typestyle and the *exact* position of the character in terms of each of the 300 dots per inch, if that is the specification of your laser printer. In addition, laser printers need to understand commands about complex graphics, which would be impossible with a daisy–wheel printer and of very poor quality on a dot–matrix printer.A laser printer is therefore required to interpret specific information relating to every single point of a page. For an A4 page a 300 dots per inch laser printer could print as many as 8,679,825 dots!

A powerful number cruncher is therefore required to cope with all of this information. Consequently, laser printers have large memories to be able to handle all the information being sent to them. Also, since each page is unique in that it is made up of a various letters in various typefaces and sizes, and may or may not include graphics within, or next to, the text, the whole process is speeded up if the computer instructs the printer in a way which describes the whole page. The computers within laser printers therefore understand something called a 'page description language'.

Anyone who performs desktop publishing can produce excellent results without ever having to learn anything about page description languages (PDLs). The desktop publishing page make–up applications automatically convert the WYSIWYG material you have worked on into the appropriate PDL, immediately prior to printing.

Not surprisingly, the most widely used PDL is the one which Apple Computers adopted for their LaserWriter printer. It is called

'PostScript'. PostScript is understood by a number of other laser printers as well, although there are other PDLs, one of which is confusingly called 'DDL' or 'Document Description Language'. This is the language understood by Hewlett Packard laser printers, and describes the entire document, rather than each individual page. However, it is possible to adapt laser printers so that they understand PostScript by adding hardware, from third party suppliers. This emphasises the importance of PostScript.

Since PostScript is so widely used, it may well be worth checking that your equipment can use it. One of its few drawbacks is that it is not the fastest page description language. PostScript can take many minutes to convert your screen image into understandable code for your printer, especially if there are complex graphics involved.

However, this time is small in comparison to the days it might have taken using traditional typesetting. Another point about the so–called slow speed of PostScript, when compared to DDL, or some other page description languages, is the fact that the speed of the printing is also dependent upon the on–board memory of the printer. If the memory is fairly small — for some pages even a couple of megabytes may be small — the conversion of the PostScript code into a printed image will take longer. The slowness of PostScript will be improved as higher RAMs become available in laser printers.

Putting the speed argument to one side, there is another reason why you might wish to opt for PostScript. This is the fact that it is understood by Linotronic typesetting machines, through a special interface known as a Raster Image Processor (RIP). Pages prepared with PostScript can be printed at high quality through a Linotronic typesetter, without the need for typesetting itself. The disks can be translated by the RIP and understood by the Linotronic typesetting machines. In this way desktop publishers can produce artwork at high resolutions of either 1,270 dots per inch or 2,400 dots per inch using either the Linotronic 100 or the Linotronic 300 machines.

These machines are widely used by typesetters, many of whom can accept disks and print off the pages from them. In this way desktop publishers can achieve typeset quality relatively cheaply — around £6 ($9) per page, and more speedily than if the material had to put together by a keyboard operator and a compositor. So using PostScript opens up the possibility of vast improvements on quality over and above laser printers. Other page description languages are expected to be able to interface with other types of typesetting equipment, so the need for PostScript may become less important in the future.

So there you have your basic desktop publishing system:

a microcomputer with at least 512k of RAM, a high resolution, paper white screen, and capable of expansion

a laser printer capable of understanding a page description language

Which manufacturer?

So what choices of hardware does this leave you with?

Apple

Until the beginning of 1987 you would have had little choice other than the Apple Macintosh system. Indeed, this held over 70 per cent of the worldwide desktop publishing market up until the beginning of 1987.

Even though industrial observers claim that this market share will half during the following years it will still be the largest selling single product with around one–third of the market — and, because of the massive interest and potential for desktop publishing, this will be a market which is more than double the size of that seen from 1986 to 1987. Consequently, the Apple Macintosh system will be in widespread use and all other systems will be measured up against it.

IBM PC and clones

However, desktop publishing programs will work on an IBM PC, although the 'AT' version, with a higher memory than the standard 256k RAM 'PC', is required. Cheaper AT compatibles are available and desktop publishing software does work on many of these.

Apricot

Another possible hardware choice is the Apricot Xen. This can run MS DOS versions of desktop publishing software with full IBM compatibility. The Apricot Xen is also a computer capable of networking and comes with a paper white monitor with high resolution graphics. Apricot, like Apple, sells a desktop publishing package of hardware and software. The only real difference between the systems being IBM compatibility. Apple is not IBM compatible. For people who need such compatibility, the Apricot may be the ideal choice for desktop publishing.

Canon

Another possibility is the Canon Personal Publishing system. This too is IBM compatible and is sold as a package including software. The difference here is that the software bundled with the computer is a unique item to Canon. Apple and Apricot desktop publishing systems utilise the same main piece of desktop publishing software, a program called 'PageMaker'. As will be seen later on in this book, PageMaker is an industry standard against which all other programs are measured. The program supplied with the Canon system is not so powerful and, although PageMaker will work on IBM compatibles, such as the Canon Personal Publisher, you would have to pay extra for it buying the Canon program as well.

Xerox

A further option is provided by Xerox — the original inventors of the term 'desktop publishing'. This company is providing a further package called 'Documentor'. This system is IBM compatible and is aimed largely at larger commercial concerns. Again, the disadvantage of this system for some users may be the software supplied in the package. It is not as well established as PageMaker. But for people who wish to produce standard, attractive, fairly complex documents, involving graphics, the system may be ideal.

Atari

The Atari 540 ST is yet another possibility. This runs the powerful and cost effective program Fleet Street Publisher. The whole system can be bought as a package with the computer which is very Macintosh–like, the program and a laser printer.

Like the Macintosh, the Atari is easy to use. It is also a cost effective solution for many people who wish to enter professional desktop publishing but for whom finances are limited.

Amstrad

Fleet Street Publisher will also run on the Amstrad PC1512 computer series. It may therefore provide a cost effective publishing set up for individuals. However, the Amstrad PC1512 does not have many expansion slots, and this could prove to be tricky if you are likely to want to add all sorts of bits and pieces to the system. The Amstrad though, is IBM compatible and therefore will run an enormous range of software.

Advent

There is also another option in the Advent series of computers and software. The system is IBM compatible, has an A4 screen as standard, unlike all of the others, but once again software will be the deciding factor for many people.

The answer is to check everything before you purchase. Apart from the hardware considerations already outlined earlier in this chapter you will want to know whether or not the system is IBM compatible (if this is important to your other work) whether the system can do exactly what you want it to do — always see it in operation before you buy and ask other users — and whether or not the system will run PageMaker. You may never need PageMaker but if your system *will* support PageMaker you will be able to use one of the most powerful computer programs available, the 'Rolls Royce' of desktop publishing.

For most general professional desktop publishing set–ups the choice for hardware is going to be between IBM PCs and compatibles, Apple, Apricot, Atari and Xerox. People with highly specific needs, such as technical documentation, may find that more dedicated systems will suit their needs, rather than one of these wide ranging options.

DeskTop Publishing System from Apple Computer, comprising the Macintosh Plus personal computer and LaserWriter printer.

Chapter 3

Publishing Basics

The vast majority of people who will be buying and using desktop publishing systems in the mid–to–late 1980s are likely to be novices to the world of publishing. People, such as personnel officers, marketing managers and so on, could all benefit from desktop publishing and many are likely to buy systems to help improve their communications. However, when considering the systems on offer and when starting to use these systems, such people will have a whole new vocabulary thrust upon them. It is therefore important to learn some of the basics of publishing so that informed choices can be made about purchasing decisions and so that the publications produced by the systems can be professional in their appearance; you will need to understand traditional publishing vocabulary to be able to talk to printers, for example.

At the end of this book is a glossary which explains the most frequently used terms in publishing. This chapter will help explain many of these words in the context of the whole process of publishing, a process which for the most part does not depend upon the technology used. Consequently the vocabulary of desktop publishing is shared with that of traditional publishing.

Publishing ideas

The very beginning of any publishing project starts with the basic idea. This could be for a 64 page daily newspaper, or a 160 page annual directory. It could be a weekly in–house newsletter of four pages, or a brochure for potential business clients. Whatever it is, you will have a concept of the sort of publication you would like to see in print.

From this basic idea starts the planning for the publication. The first question which needs to be answered during publication planning is 'what will the publication cover?' or 'what will its content be?' The answers to this will be different according to the type of publication. If it is to be a staff newsletter, for example, the content could be about the successes of the company with snippets of news about the staff. If it is a brochure it may be about the whole company, or just about one of its products. If it is to be a monthly magazine, will it contain any news items, for example. The initial stages of planning will look at all of the possibilities for the content and will probably lead to a number of different ideas. In large publishing houses all of these ideas are considered before making a final decision as to which one to accept. Anyone involved in desktop publishing should take note of the hundreds of years of publishing experience and consider a wide range of options for each publication before starting work on it. Don't just launch into the production of an annual report for the company without, for example, considering whether or not a half yearly report might be more appropriate, or would a monthly magazine be better.

Should the report be aimed at shareholders, or customers? Should it contain views from the staff? Will it contain photographs or drawings? Will it be 'newsy' or will it contain long feature style articles? These are the sorts of questions which need to be answered after coming up with a basic idea and *before* starting any work on the publication. You will be amazed at the number of people, including traditional publishers, who produce a publication and then change their mind about what it should contain. This only serves to confuse your readers and can therefore be damaging.

Having made a decision about the publication and its overall content, including whether or not you will accept advertising, the next important decision to make relates to the frequency of publication — how often will it be produced? In many instances this may well relate to the overall costs of publication, as well as to the type of material being published. For example, a newspaper needs to be published fairly frequently, otherwise the content becomes 'stale'. However, a directory may need to be published every year, or only once. A book, such as this one, may only need one publication, although occasional updates may become necessary from time to time.

If you are producing a company newsletter you will need to consider the amount of time available to do the work, the costs of producing the material, as well as the expectations of the staff as to how often they would like to see the publication. Many matters like these will need to be considered before you can go on to the next stage of publication planning — scheduling.

Scheduling

Scheduling is one of the most important aspects of any publication. However, producing a production schedule is not always the easiest task, since it involves so many variables. A schedule is a list of dates which shows when certain stages of production of the publication are reached. The final date on any such production schedule is the date of distribution.

This should be the *starting* date for designing any production schedule. Start at the bottom with the date you want the material to be in the hands of the readers and work upwards from there. A typical production schedule (see Figure 1) for a publication includes the date at which the production of the written material or 'copy' starts and ends; the dates between which this copy is edited; the dates on which the layouts will be prepared, headlines, picture captions, and so on, written; the dates on which the pages are read for errors and corrected; the date on which the final master pages are sent to the printer; the date when the printer will deliver the printed editions of the publication; and finally the date when the material will be distributed.

1. Copy due	15th April
2. Editing by	20th April
3. Pass to subs	21st April
4. Subbing finished by	26th April
5. Layouts completed by	28th April
6. Typesetting completed by	9th May
7. Check proofs by	12th May
8. Second proofs delivered by	16th May
9. Final corrections by	18th May
10. Pass for Press	21st May
11. Printing starts	23rd May
12. Delivery	30th May

Figure 1 — A typical production schedule

All of these dates will need careful working out. If you are producing the publication alone and only need co-ordinate with a printer, the job is obviously going to be a lot easier than if a whole team of individuals has to be fitted in with the schedule. The schedule is also complicated further if your publication is to accept advertising, since potential advertisers will need to be contacted and given time to produce the artwork for their adverts well in advance of you putting the publication together.

Flatplans

Once a schedule is produced the next stage of publication production is the 'editorial plan'. Publications which accept advertising start the editorial plan with a 'flatplan' of the advertising which will show the size and position of each advertisement in the publication (See Figure 2). This is very important since many advertisers buy 'special positions' to give their advertisement prominence, such as the back cover or inside the front page. These special positions cost more than advertisements which are placed anywhere within the publication and therefore the publication must be printed with them where the advertiser wanted them! Some magazines also offer advertisers a spot in the 'front half' of the publication.

Research has shown that the first half of many publications has more readers than the second half. So advertisers are sometimes charged a higher fee for appearing in the first half where their advertisement will be spotted by a higher number of people. All of these considerations need to be taken into account when producing a publication which contains advertising, so the advertising flatplan is the basis upon which the magazine, or newspaper, is put together. An advertising flatplan is also important in one other respect, it helps decide the total number of pages.

Publications which accept advertising, rely heavily on the income from the advertisers to pay printing bills. So, with fewer advertisements, the publisher has less cash to finance print bills. Most commercial publishers therefore print fewer pages when advertisements are low in number.

However, it is not just a simple matter of deciding the number of pages for which the advertisements are likely to pay. As will be seen

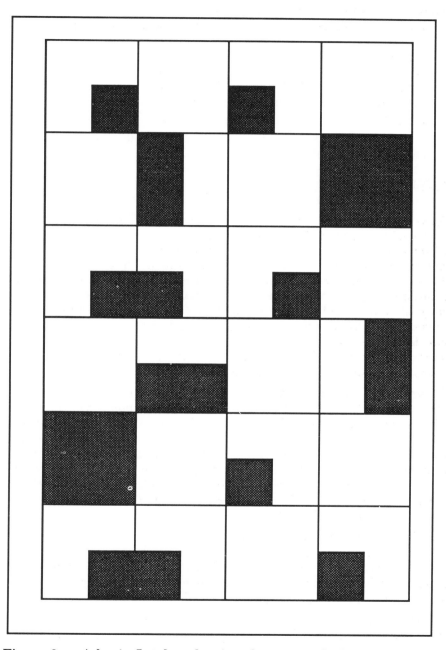

Figure 2 — A basic flatplan showing the areas which will contain advertising as shaded blocks

later in this chapter, 'pagination' — the total number of pages in an issue — depends upon a number of factors, including the type of printing–machine used by the printer. This is one item which needs to be considered when deciding on the number of pages the publication will be. An advertising flatplan will also show the publisher the 'ad-ed' ratio. This is the ratio of advertisement space to the space remaining for editorial.

The figures are expressed as '60-40', for example, meaning that 60 per cent of the publication is advertising whilst 40 per cent is editorial matter. The right balance must be struck, so that the publication does not look like it is purely advertising, or that it contains so much editorial it is costly to produce. An ad-ed ratio of 60-40 is very common in magazine publishing, especially in magazines which are distributed free of charge, although higher and lower ratios can be seen.

So the editorial plan begins with the flatplan. This is a drawing of the whole publication in miniature on one sheet of paper. Programs such as PageMaker allow you to produce flatplans which can show the positioning of adverts, standard items, such as logos and so on. PageMaker calls this a 'thumbnails' picture. Thumbnails are basically miniature representations of each page and are often used in traditional publishing to sketch out ideas.

Editorial planning

With a thumbnail picture of a publication, or its flatplan, real editorial planning can begin. The overall editorial plan will decide where each sort of written material will be placed. For example, the publication may have some news items, which are generally placed in the first few pages, then it might have feature articles, regular columns, and so on.

The names of all of these items are written on the flatplan so that everyone involved with the publication knows exactly what type of copy will appear on each page. Having produced this master plan, more detailed planning takes place. This is where editors decide which 'stories' or 'pieces' — journalistic shorthand for written material — will go on each page. In this way a structure for the publication evolves during the planning process and no-one should be in any doubt as to what goes where.

This sort of planning is essential, no matter what type of publication is being produced. Whether it is a daily newspaper or an annual report, it is vital that whoever is producing it knows what material is intended for each page. It is no use getting all of the material together and then trying to produce the publication. Either you will end up with more copy than you can fit in the number of pages you can afford to print, or you will have a number of blank pages and will have to rush for material because the printer is screaming for the artwork!

Copy Production

Once the major editorial plan is produced and the publisher, or editor, knows what type of material is on which page, the copy can be produced. Because the flatplan reveals how much space there is for a particular item it is possible to determine how much needs to be written.

For example, there may be four pages of news in a publication and, depending on the size of paper used and the size of type, a publisher will know how many stories and how many words will be needed to fill the space available. This sort of calculation is an essential part of traditional publishing, since it avoids articles being too short, or too long. It is important too in office based publishing. If the annual report is to be 48 pages long, it is no good producing enough written material for 54 since a lot of difficult cutting will be needed. Similarly, it would be a problem trying to make only 40 pages worth of copy fit into the 48 pages available. You would then need extra time to produce the additional material. Only by careful editorial planning will such problems be avoided. No matter what type of publication a desktop publisher wishes to produce, editorial planning is vital. This book, for example went through a number of planning stages before a single word was committed to paper (well, *screen* in actual fact). It was only once the overall plan of the whole book, then individual plans of each chapter had been produced, was any copy written.

After all of the planning and the production of flatplans, schedules and editorial plans, the actual task of copy production can begin. For regular publications such as newspapers and magazines, obviously, copy is produced almost continuously. However, for other publications, such as books, reports, brochures, proposals and so on, copy production is a one–off affair.

This means that copy production really only starts after the final editorial plan is produced. However, for on–going publications a supply of copy will become available for each issue as more copy is produced in the run–up to the production of the editorial plan. The knowledge of the availability of this copy is taken into account when producing the plan and such articles are incorporated into the issue in question. This means that such publications will be able to partly 'fill' each issue at the flatplan stage and therefore reducing the requirement for further copy immediately.

Copy is produced according to the schedule. Large publications such as magazines and newspapers have different copy deadlines for different parts of each issue. In this way the publication can be gradually built up with the most recent and newsworthy material being put together last of all. In an office situation this may be a necessary requirement in newsletters for example, but is unlikely to occur in other forms of office publishing. A difference between desktop publishing and traditional publishing is, as already mentioned, the vast improvement of speed with the new technology. This means that 'closing sections' does not usually occur.

Closing a section in traditional publishing, means that a batch of pages has to be completed earlier than other parts of the publication in order to allow time for all of the typesetting. Magazines often have a number of different sections which are processed separately to allow enough time for the long process of typesetting.

With desktop publishing this is not a problem, and consequently late items can be included anywhere within the publication. In most newspapers and magazines such items can only be included in the front pages since these are generally in the last section to close.

Once all the copy is provided editing takes place. This is where the editor, or publisher, decides whether or not the stories planned for the publication are still relevant; whether they have been written well; whether or not they are accurate, honest, fair and legal; and whether or not more work, or a different 'angle', is required. An angle is the factual viewpoint from which the copy is written.

Sub–Editing

Once all of these decisions have been made the next stage of the publication process can take place. This is called 'sub–editing' or 'subbing'. A 'sub' is a senior journalist whose job is to check every single word of the copy. The copy is checked for grammar and spelling as well as for accuracy, interest and 'house style'. Every publication should have a house style and all desktop publishers should adopt their own — and even produce their own booklet describing the house style.

A house style booklet would contain information on a number of different items, including such things as the number of columns the publication has and how they may be varied; the maximum size of headline type allowed; the typeface to be used for captions of photographs; and textual information such as the fact that 'per cent' is always spelled out, and never put in as %, or that numbers up to and including ten are always written in full but 11 and over can be numerals, or that contractions such as Dr and Mrs do not have full stops after them but abbreviations like Rev. or Prof. always have them. All major publications have their own style book and *The Economist* has even published its version for anyone to use (see Bibliography).

Once a sub has gone through the copy, and altered it to make sure it is acceptable for publication, it will then be 'counted' and 'measured'. The sub will count the number of words or individual characters in the copy and then calculate how long it will be in a given size and typeface for a given 'column width'. A page layout, usually produced by other sub editors, will have on it a space for the particular story. This space might be say ten inches but the sub may calculate the copy to be 12 inches. The sub therefore has to go back through the copy and cut out two inches worth of words! If the article is 'short', the sub will have to write more copy, or get the original author to write more.

Once the page layout is complete and all of the copy is thought to fit properly the material is sent to a typesetter. All of the copy will have been typed by a writer. Once it is at the typesetter somebody types it into another keyboard all over again!

The keyboard the typesetter uses is linked to a computer and the codes which a typesetter inserts into the copy tell the typesetting equipment information about the typeface and the size and so on. The machine then produces the typeset material as a 'bromide', a long strip of paper with the typeset material on it. All of the bromides for a publication are collectively called 'galleys'.

Once the galleys are produced the compositor cuts them up and sticks them on the page according to the sub's roughly drawn layout, together with any other material such as logos, pictures and so on. These pages are then photocopied and the 'proofs' returned to the publishers for checking. Naturally, since the calculations performed by the subs are not going to be exact every time, some of the typeset material will be too long for the space allotted to it, whilst other stories will be too short. During the first checking stage the subs readjust the page to make it 'fit' and check for any spelling mistakes, or 'literals' as they are called. Once this proof reading is performed, the corrected proofs are returned to the typesetters, who carry out all of the changes and return 'final proofs' to the publishers for approval. Only then can the material be 'passed for press'. This means that the publisher agrees on the fact that the pages are acceptable for printing and publication.

It is this to-ing and fro-ing in the traditional publishing process, which does not occur with desktop publishing, which is the point at which most time–saving occurs. In desktop publishing the production of copy can be done at the same time as the layout of the page. Therefore the stories can be written to fit exactly the space allotted to them. Most of the powerful page layout programs also have their own spelling checkers, meaning that literals can be avoided too. This means that the first pages printed by a laser printer can also be the final pages, already passed for press.

Printing

Once the whole process of producing material for publication is complete there is the problem of printing and 'finishing'. Many people are misled into believing that a laser printer can act as a printing machine for multiple copies of the same document. Whilst this is perfectly possible it is not advisable. The laser printer will only be able to produce about 110,000 copies in its lifetime of around three years. Once this level of production has been reached the photocopier–like 'engine' needs replacement. An additional problem is that the quantity of toner is important in producing a consistent image on all documents. As more pages are produced toner is used up, which means that for a long print run the last copies could be less clear than the earlier ones. The way to avoid all this trouble and extend the likely life of your laser printer, thus saving money, is to use the laser printer to produce master pages, which are then passed on to a commercial printer.

Not only will this process help reduce overall costs by extending the life of the laser printer, but it will also produce a better printed batch of documents since quality is more likely to be consistent. Obviously, if you are only going to print a handful of copies you need not bother with commercial printing, but any fair sized document which is produced in a print run of more than 100 really ought to be done by a commercial printer. High street copy shops can provide good quality printing services for short run publications and there are many printers who will now accept material from desktop publishers for long run publications.

One thing which desktop publishing manuals do not tell you is the range of printing options which are available to anyone using laser printer output as 'camera ready copy ' (CRC). The most widespread printing process available today is called 'offset lithography'. The basic principle can be used on small machines to print, say, 250 copies of a letterhead, or on massive rotary machines printing half a million copies of a glossy colour magazine.

Litho printing is similar to the process used in laser printing. The areas to be printed are treated chemically so that they accept ink and repell water. Those areas which are to remain unprinted — the white spaces — will repell ink and accept water. The master page is made into a plate, a metal copy of the page to be printed. This is made from a 'film'. This is literally a photograph of the page and can either be a negative, or a positive, just as in 35mm transparency photography. However, in printing, the film is large enough to carry a copy of the full size page on it. This is then used to make a print on the plates. When these are made the chemicals are used to treat the printing and non–printing areas. The plate is then covered with ink and water and pressed against the paper. Ink will only be on those areas where letters and so on are present.

Offset lithography depends upon this litho process, but does not print directly to paper. Instead it prints the image from the inked plate to a piece of rubber. The paper is pressed against the rubber, rather than the metal plate. Paper is very rough if you look at it under a microscope. This roughness can damage the expensive metal plates and for long print runs they, therefore, have to be produced more frequently, increasing the cost of printing. Using pieces of rubber to 'offset' the paper from the metal plate means that the plates last longer, thus cutting costs.

Printers use different kinds of printing machines for different print 'jobs'. Each separate publication for printing is a 'job'. Some jobs will only require small printing machines, such as 1,000 copies of a company brochure. Whereas, long run magazines will require larger machines which are 'web fed'. A 'web' is a large roll of paper, which is rolled through a machine, enabling a number of pages to be printed at one time, and both sides of the paper to be printed upon at the same time. This saves a considerable amount of printing time, and is therefore a cheaper method of printing.

However, web–offset printing requires investment in capital equipment of millions of pounds or dollars. Small print runs are generally dealt with by 'sheet fed' printers. These will only print on one sheet of paper at a time. The sheets are generally large pieces of paper and can therefore contain a number of pages on them. However, only expensive sheet fed printers can print on both sides at the same time, meaning that once one side of the publication is printed the paper has to be turned over and passed through the printing machine once more. This slows down the printing process and is therefore more costly.

Desktop publishers need to know what process a printer uses. The reason is that it may influence the cost of producing a publication from the laser printer master pages. A publication, which could economically be printed on a web machine, is going to cost more if your printer only has a sheet fed press.

It is therefore essential to get a number of quotes from different printers for all print jobs. How to get such quotes is dealt with later in this chapter. Before you can obtain such quotes you will need to be clear about a number of other factors on the printing of your publication. Will it contain any colour material? If so, is it just 'spot colour' or 'four colour'.

Colour Printing

Printing–machines only print in four colours. These are black, yellow, magenta, and cyan. A colour photograph, for example, when printed in a magazine, or brochure, only contains these four colours. The various combinations of the four inks give rise to the differing shades. If you are to use four colour pictures in publications the pictures will need 'separating'. This is an electronic process which produces four sheets of film for each colour picture. Each film represents the amount of each colour of ink which will be attracted to the printing areas of the plate. Sophisticated offset printing–machines can print all four colours in one 'pass' or run through the machine. Other printing–machines can only deal with one colour of ink at a time and therefore four colour printing requires four passes through the machine. This too will obviously affect overall printing costs.

Spot colours are where logos, lines, words and so on are printed in one colour only. If only one spot colour is required, such as magenta or cyan, then the costs of printing are reduced. Other spot colours can be chosen and there is a specially prepared range of pre-mixed inks called 'Pantones'. Each ink is defined as a Pantone Number and publishers can specify exact colours for their areas of spot colour by quoting a Pantone Number.

Imposition

Another consideration in printing a publication is imposition. Because each printing machine can print a number of pages at one time, and often can print on both sides of the paper at the same time, pages will not be placed on the plate in consecutive order. They will be 'imposed' in an order so that once the printed paper is folded and cut all of the pages are *then* in the correct order. Most printing—machines work in a combination of pages, in fours, eights, 16s or 32s. Depending on the type of printing—machine used, and where folds and cuts in the paper are to appear, the pages will be in a specific order on the plate. Figure 3 shows a few examples of imposition.

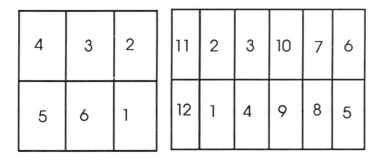

Figure 3 — Two different types of imposition, showing that publications do not appear on a printed sheet in the order they will be read!

Once a printer knows how many pages of what size your publication is going to be, how many copies you want, how many colours will be required and where folds will occur (some brochures, for example, may have unusual folding requirements) only two other basic items of information are required. The printer will need to know what type of paper is required and the 'finishing' wanted.

Paper

Paper comes in a wide variety. You can have a number of colours; it can be thin, fairly thick, glossy or matt. All of these differences obviously affect price and will need to be considered when planning any desktop publication.

The first thing to consider is the colour required. White paper is generally the cheapest, although bright white papers do need special treatment to produce the pure effect and can therefore cost extra. Coloured papers are also obviously more expensive.

After colour, the next consideration is weight. Paper comes in a variety of different weights. A heavy paper is thicker than a light paper. In the UK the weight of any paper is measured in the number of grams each square metre of one sheet of the paper actually weighs. This is expressed as 'gsm'. A newspaper may be something like 60gsm. In the United States, however, paper weights are dealt with differently. The Americans classify paper weight in terms of the number of pounds 500 sheets of paper the print machine uses would weigh. Sadly, too the Americans do not use the international standards of the 'A series', but have their own classification. Basically, though, the higher the weight of paper you will use the better the quality. Most magazine are printed on something like 120gsm paper, which should give you an idea of the sort of weight you may require for your publication. Photocopier paper, at the lower end of the scale, is around 70gsm. Once you get up to around 200gsm you are printing on lightweight card.

However, the weight of the paper is not the only consideration. Do you want it glossy or matt? Do you want cheap or more costly paper? Cheap newsletters and magazines or leaflets can be printed on 'mechanical paper'. This is used largely on web–offset machines.

However, greater quality is achieved with 'coated' papers. These papers are covered with clay and then rolled under heavy pressure. The coating then sticks to the paper and gives it a gloss. However, there are also coated papers which are not glossy but have a smooth matt finish. Such paper is called 'blade coated cartridge'. This is ideal for company brochures, annual reports, newsletters and so on. When deciding on the sort of paper for any publication be sure that the printer can handle such paper and has either got stocks in hand or can easily obtain the paper. Paper prices vary enormously and obtaining a small amount of paper for a single publication can be extremely expensive. When asking for print quotes always get the printer to let you know of any near alternatives to your requirements, since what the printer has available may work out considerably cheaper, yet still provide you with the quality you require.

Finishing

Once you have decided upon the paper the only remaining item which a printer will need to know about, other than minor details about delivery dates and where to send the printed material, will be 'finishing'. The whole process of finishing includes a variety of items such as cutting, folding, 'collating' and binding. When the paper comes out of the printing machine it will have all of the pages of the publication joined together. These will need to be separated from each other by cutting and folding. So, for example a four page newsletter will have pages two and three printed next to each other, with pages one and four printed on their backs.

However, this means that each sheet of paper will only have two pages on each side. To make it economical the printer will put a number of copies of the publication on the same sheet of paper. A small printing–machine could carry, say, four copies of a four page newsletter. Therefore the paper would need cutting into four blocks, which would then need folding correctly to make up the four page newsletter.

When the folding is done there will be rough edges in places, and the paper will be larger than the actual size of the publication — the paper used by the printing–machine, obviously, has to have a border to grip so that the material can be passed through the machine. The excess paper is then trimmed from the folded pages.

If the publication consists of more than one folded sheet the pages will need assembling in the correct order. This assembly is called 'collating'. Most printers have machines to do this autmoatically, but if you go to a small print firm they may need to do it by hand, so this could increase costs. Once all of the pages have been collated, then they can be bound or stitched. There are a variety of bindings available and all have their different uses, with various advantages and disadvantages. Newsletters, for example, do not need to be bound but they sometimes need to be stitched.

A stitch is generally a staple, also known as a 'saddle stitch'. However, some publications can be stitched with cotton, though saddle stitching is more common and usually cheaper.

If a publication needs to be bound there are a variety of options. One is called 'perfect binding', where a number of groups of pages are joined together. Each group is called a 'signature'. The signatures can be stitched together, then glued to the cover. A similar process occurs with case binding. This is when the publication has a stiff cover, as in a hardback book, and is more expensive. This book is case bound.

Other types of binding available for publications include ring binders, plastic gripper bindings, wire bindings and so on. Cheap machines for office based binding can be bought and these are useful for desktop publishing operations in commercial concerns, where only a few copies of each publication are being printed by the laser printer.

Once a printer knows what is required all that remains to be covered is the delivery date and where the material is to be sent to once it is printed. A printer needs to know a precise delivery date. This is why publishers produce schedules for each publication which details the delivery date. Printing machines are very expensive. If a printer leaves them idle for any length of time he will not be recouping his capital investment.

Consequently, a printer needs to know when each publication is required by a publisher, so that its printing can be slotted in to the schedule of use of the printing–machines. For this reason it is important to deliver CRCs to a printer by the specified date. If you do not the printer may have to leave the machine free of work until your CRCs arrive. If this happens you will be charged 'wait time'. This can very expensive, so be warned!

Another warning which all desktop publishers should remember is: consider storage space! It may be an excellent idea to produce 1,000 copies of an A4 company brochure of 48 pages. But that will need roughly the equivalent space to 100 boxes of typing paper. Publishing 500 copies of your own hardback book on your favourite hobby may be a long cherished dream but they could fill up your garage! Desktop publishers should not wait until the articulated lorry arrives from the printers before thinking about where to put the delivery!

Getting a delivery of a publication from a printer is exciting but all publishers need to converse in the same language as printers if the products delivered are to be the ones which the publisher wanted. Anyone new to publishing should therefore be sure they understand the printing process, as described in this chapter.

The language of publication production is vital to any desktop publisher. This is the reason why the language of traditional publishing has been adopted by the companies making desktop publishing software.

House Style

During the editorial planning of any publication, as described earlier in this chapter, a number of decisions need to be taken about the overall look of the product. These may include such things as whether it will contain any spot colour or even four colour artwork, the size of the page and so on. However, also discussed during editorial planning will be the various typographic choices available. For many publishers these are defined in the written house style. However, for new publishers, especially those involved in desktop publishing, decisions need to be made from scratch. In Chapter 6 we shall be looking at how to make those choices but first you will need to understand the vocabulary which page make–up programs use to provide you with the various options. The vocabulary, as already mentioned is the same as that used by traditional typesetters. Most of the words are listed in the glossary at the end of this book but the important ones are dealt with here.

The first option any publisher has is deciding the number of columns there will be on each page. Once this decision is made a page grid can be produced showing the outlines of the columns but only if the actual size of each column is known. Printers measure width on pages in terms of units called 'pica ems'. A pica em is the width of a capital letter 'M' which measures 12 'points'. A point is a fraction of an inch. In desktop publishing terms there are exactly 72 points to each inch. In traditional typesetting there are fractionally more (72.06 points to the inch). However, the difference is minimal and of no real relevance. Printers always measure width in pica ems (12 point units), but height in terms of points only. An individual column is, therefore, said to be so many points by so many pica ems. The gap between columns, the 'gutter', is also measured in pica ems.

Type is measured in points. When instructing typesetter, or choosing type on a desktop publishing system, a publisher will decide that 'body copy', the main text, will be in type of a particular point size. The type on this page is set in 12 point. The height of any text is measured from the top of the 'ascenders' (the parts of the text above the line as in a 'b' or an 'h' or a 'd') to the bottom of the 'descenders' (the parts of the text below the line as in a 'y' or a 'j' or a 'p')(see Figure 4). Another aspect of type size is called 'leading' (pronounced 'ledding'). This is the distance, measured in points, between the bottom of one line of text to the bottom of the next line of text (see Figure 5). Most publications insert a small amount of space between each line of text. If not, descenders on one line run into the risk of joining up with the ascenders on the line below. This may be why type set without any space between the lines is known as 'solid' type.

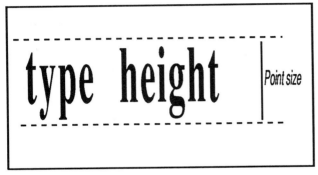

Figure 4 — Point size is measured from the top of ascenders to the bottom of descenders

The distance between the bottom margins of lines of text is generally larger than the typesize itself. For example, this text is set in 10 point (pt) with an 11pt leading. This is referred to as 10 on 11, or more simply 10/11pt. Desktop publishing programs allow you to choose the size of the type and also to control the leading. This will of course depend upon the type of publication you are producing and the effect you are attempting to achieve. But it should be remembered that as the column width reduces the size of type needs to be reduced too.

Narrow newspaper columns, for example, can comfortably use 8/9 type. But books, with wider column measures, need something like 10/11 or 11/12 to be read easily. There are various methods of calculating the exact size of type required, depending upon the width of a column. It is also possible to determine the ideal width for a particular size of type. In general, type of 9/10 and 10/11 pts will be most easily readable over columns of 15 pica ems. This is equivalent to three columns on an A4 page.

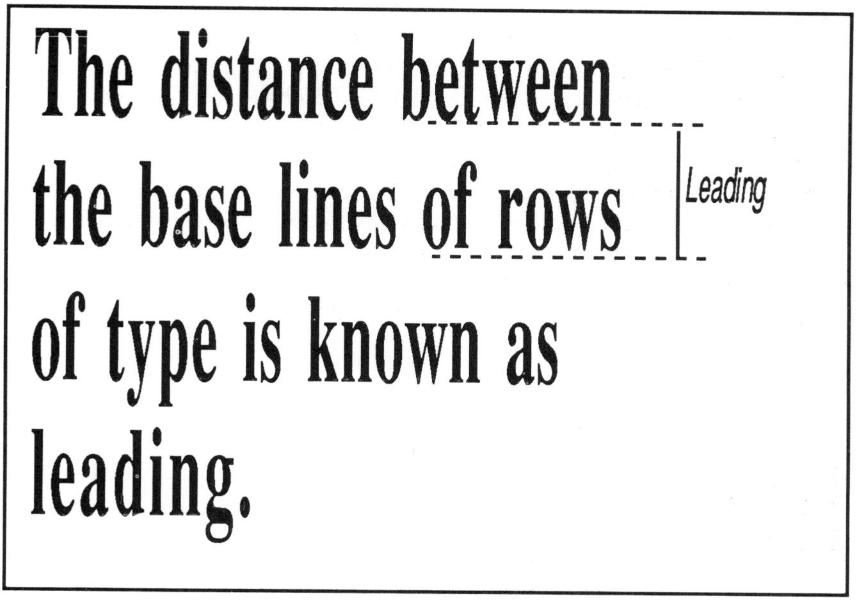

The distance between the base lines of rows of type is known as leading.

Leading

Figure 5 — Leading is the distance between rows of type

Column width, type size and leading are not the only matters which require understanding for publication production. There are also the various typefaces. There are many thousands of different versions available with different names. This book is set in a face called 'New Century Schoolbook'. Newspapers use a face commonly referred to as 'Times'. Typesetting machines can produce a wide variety of different typefaces. So can laser printers, and it is even possible to design your own!

However, typefaces are not all the same. Times produced by one typesetting machine will not be exactly the same as that produced by another. The characters will have very slightly differing designs and the shape of the body of each character may also differ. Consequently the alphabet of Times from one machine in 12pt may measure 10 pica ems, whereas from another it would measure 11pica ems. Laser printers from different manufacturers may produce a slight variations in typefaces. If you are to use more than one brand of laser printer in an office, for example, note carefully if there are any differences in typefaces as this may affect your publication's appearance.

Typefaces can also be produced in a numer of different styles. They can be set bold, for example, or italic. They can be set 'light', which is less heavy than the normal 'Roman', the term often used to signify standard type for a particular face. In reality, though, Roman is the standard for Times. Typefaces can also be printed extended, condensed, or oblique (almost italic). Most of these options are available in desktop publishing. However, most desktop publishing programs have other added options, such as shadow or outlined text. These are effects which should be generally avoided. As will be seen in later chapters they are not very useful in terms of publication design and many desktop publications have 'overused' such textual tricks.

Once you have decided on a typeface, its style and size you have defined a 'fount' (pronounced 'font' — and spelt that way in the US). For example the fount you currently see on the page is 10 on 11 point New Century Schoolbook. Some people will incorrectly describe 'New Century Schoolbook' as a fount. It is not, it is a face. Only when the size *and* face are given have you chosen a fount.

Another point about type is that it comes, largely, in two main versions. these are called 'serif' and 'sanserif'. A serif is a little curl at the end of a line. So serif faces do not have straight edges. Like the face you are reading now, the characters of serif fonts have little curls on the edges, whereas sanserif faces are without the curled edges (see Figure 6). Sanserif faces are straight and are less easily read than serif faces and, as will be seen later, should generally be avoided for long portions of text. Sanserif faces are much better utilised as display type for headlines.

All the words introduced so far are those referred to in desktop publishing programs and manuals. Other words will be introduced later on and are listed in the glossary. However, the above basics should be enough for anyone new to the world of publishing to be able to understand the terminology, as well as see the immense similarities between desktop publishing and the traditional techniques.

Publication Design

Endless amounts of research have gone in to publication design which all shows that well–designed and attractively laid out publications tend to get more readers than those publications which appear to be thrown together. Sadly, many people who have been

Serif type faces have curly edges

Sanserif type faces are straight

Figure 6 — The differences between the two main variants of type

involved in producing desktop publications have no experience of publication design and may therefore have produced some poor efforts. Later chapters in this book will show how to produce attractive publications from a desktop publishing program. However, a few basics will not come amiss here.

The first rule is simplicity. Try to keep each page as simple as possible. Too many columns for the width of the paper, or column widths of different proportions, tend to confuse the eye and make the publication look unattractive and difficult to read. Too many words on a page can also be off–putting, as can unclear headlining or sectioning. Too many typefaces and founts is also confusing. A good rule of thumb is to use only one basic typeface, such as Times Roman, for body copy and two or three others for headlines, sub–headings, and so on. No page should ever have more than three different typefaces upon it.

Textual tricks such as outlining and shadowing the text should also be avoided. They confuse the reader's eye, and are, therefore, most likely to make people turn over without reading! For the same reason pages should not be cluttered with design tricks such as 'shadow boxes', or 'WOBS'. A shadow box is a portion of text which is boxed off by rules of unequal width. This has the effect of lifting the box off the page casting a shadow behind (see Figure 7). A WOB is a 'white on black', text which is 'reversed out', being white text on a black background (see Figure 8). Too many of these can reduce the attractiveness of publications.

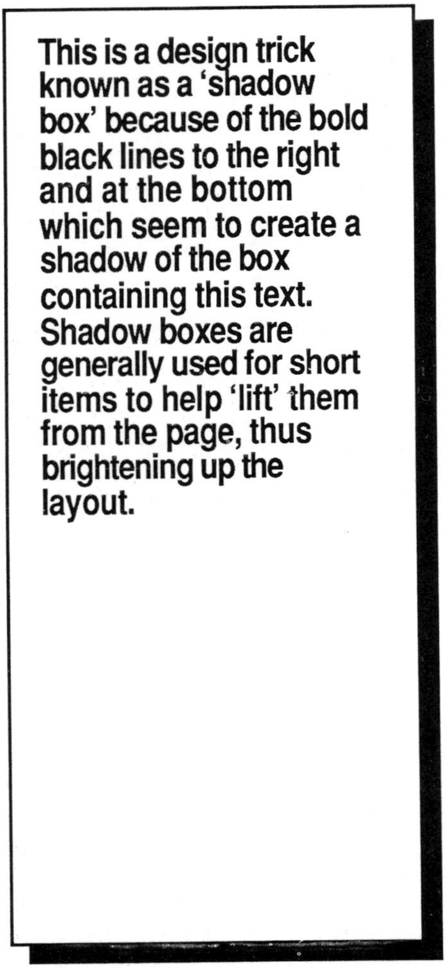

This is a design trick known as a 'shadow box' because of the bold black lines to the right and at the bottom which seem to create a shadow of the box containing this text. Shadow boxes are generally used for short items to help 'lift' them from the page, thus brightening up the layout.

Figure 7 — A shadow box

The answer for anyone trying to learn publication design is to look at the publications around you. Analyse how they are designed. You will be amazed at the simplicity and lack of 'trickery'— more of this in later chapters. There are also some excellent books on publication design listed in the bibliography.

Figure 8 — A WOB

Summary

The above discussion should have given you some idea of the basics of publishing. Publishing starts with an idea, goes through various stages of planning, including design and typography, and ends up with the printer delivering the long awaited boxes containing the publication. The process is no different for desktop publishers. All they are doing is avoiding the delays which typesetting incurs, as well as gaining increased control over the way the publication appears. How they do that is shown in the next chapter.

Chapter 4

Organising for Desktop Publishing

Having made a decision to enter the fascinating world of desktop publishing, and having thought of possible publications which could be produced using a system, some consideration will have to be given to the sort of hardware and software which will be most appropriate to your needs. If you already have a computer the decision will need to be twofold. Firstly, will the hardware you currently own be able to run desktop publishing programs with relative ease, or secondly, should you purchase replacement hardware, which will cope with desktop publishing as well as service your existing computer needs easily? For some individuals who wish to enter desktop publishing there may be no choice but to replace the hardware.

Choosing hardware is, in actual fact, the least of your worries when entering the world of desktop publishing. Choosing the right programs is much more complex. The program most suited to your needs should be sought first, then you should look for the hardware on which it will run. For most people who have an IBM or compatible the problems will only be those of upgrading to reach the requirements of desktop publishing as already outlined — high resolution graphics capable screens, at least 512k of RAM and so on.

Computer dealers will naturally enough try to sell you the hardware first, as that is where they make their money. Do not be tempted by the claims of excellent speed, or the ability to run the whole program backwards whilst tap dancing and singing the national anthem. Claims for computers are made with the sole aim of selling the machines, and there seems to be an unnecessary fixation with processor speed. It is true that the faster you can get a program to do what you ask is a good thing. But does it really matter that you can alter a typeface in 1.2 seconds with system X but only 1.9 seconds with system A? Of course not. To alter a typeface using traditional typesetting technology could take up a whole day of a publisher's time with material being sent to and fro between the typesetter and the publishing house. Fractions of a second in comparing desktop publishing hardware become superfluous.

Most of the powerful computers required to operate desktop publishing software operate at relatively high processor speeds and certainly with the speed which most operators require. So concentrate on what the programs do and how useful they will be to you, before you start worrying about the hardware. All computer magazines and journals will warn potential purchasers to ask for a demonstration of the software before opting to buy. This may not be so important with some of the basic software, which has been well documented and reviewed. However, with the complex and powerful page make-up programs used in desktop publishing a full and thorough demonstration from someone who knows how to use the product is essential. Go to a specialist dealer, who has a reputation in desktop publishing, ask people already involved in desktop publishing for advice or contact the various computer user groups for information. Some of the most well–known dealers are listed in Chapter 8.

Dealers who are not used to talking about desktop publishing software may not be able to fully answer questions, such as are there any limitations to the number of founts available, or can you precisely control leading? These are very important factors in the world of publishing. If you buy a program, which cannot do these things to the extent you would have liked, you might have to ponder whether or not the dealer actually understood your questions. After all, dealers try to sell computers, they are not attempting to be publishers. So read reviews, ask users, check brochures and so on, until you are thoroughly satisfied with the program before buying it.

Desktop publishing software is in the top price brackets for computer programs; an error therefore may be an expensive one. Choose a couple of respected dealers and ask for a number of programs to be demonstrated by each dealer. Only then will you be able to make a satisfactory choice of software for your needs. Much of the following sections of this chapter should also help you form some basic decisions about choosing desktop publishing software.

For most desktop publishers a true WYSIWYG program working on a paper white screen is essential but there are two programs worthy of note which are not WYSIWYG. Both of these programs are excellent wordprocessing programs in their own right but they offer a wide range of desktop publishing facilities, which you would normally only expect to find in a WYSIWYG page make–up program.

NewsWriter

The first of the two non—mainstream desktop publishing programs is 'NewsWriter.' This is a program developed by a British company and as such is one of the few UK desktop publishing packages around. It is probably most useful in an office publishing environment, for use by people who have little or no design experience and who do not wish to learn this task. It is, therefore, ideally suited for use in secretarial departments, since the program will automatically layout any written material entered into it into standard documents already pre-programmed.

These pre-programmed document layouts can be specifically designed for each user, or each individual user has the option of creating their own designs. However, the fact that designs, standard layouts and so on, can be pre-defined means that the program appears to the user to be nothing more than a powerful wordprocessor.

NewsWriter is much more than that and is also an ideal system for front end newspaper production. It would mean that journalists could enter their copy direct into a system so that sub—editors could play around with the design, leaving the journalists to get on with the job of creative writing. That is the essential difference between NewsWriter and most of the other desktop publishing software. NewsWriter is very much a writer's program, leaving decisions about design to be made by others, if necessary (although it does allow writers to precisely control design too).

NewsWriter has all the usual requirements for desktop publishing including hyphenation and justification as well as precise fount selection, control over leading and column widths.

Hyphenation and justification is a necessary part of any desktop publishing program. Many publications appear with each line of text in equal in width to all of the other lines in the column. The text on this page is justified. With narrow columns, as might appear on a newsletter or in a newspaper, justification can lead to large white spaces between the words to help fill out the column. These white spaces are reduced if words can be broken with a hyphen and carried over from one line to the next. This hyphenation is best done automatically by desktop publishing programs. They use a hyphenation dictionary which checks the most appropriate places for words to 'break' with a hyphen. The best programs also allow the operators to override this dictionary to alter hyphenation where word breaks appear ridiculous, replacing a hyphen elsewhere in the word.

NewsWriter allows operators to hyphenate automatically and manually. Like all other desktop publishing software, NewsWriter also allows columns to be unjustified — where each line of text is of a different width within each column. NewsWriter will also make your pages fit automatically, something which some other programs cannot do. For example, if you are producing an eight page document, such as a proposal, NewsWriter will tell you when you come to print that the document is 8.25 pages long. You can then instruct NewsWriter to make the material fit eight pages. NewsWriter automatically shaves off tiny amounts of leading throughout the publication to remove the 0.25 page excess, thus making your document a perfect fit. It can also add increments of leading to expand a document, which is short!

It may sound complicated, but the whole process only takes two keystrokes and consequently is an easy task. In fact, NewsWriter is one of the most user–friendly document processors available but there is one limitation. Other than simple graphics, such as lines and boxes, NewsWriter is unable to incorporate complex pictorial material directly but it is perfectly possible to layout the pages with spaces for pictorial material to be placed on the master laser printouts later on at the printing stage.

NewsWriter is available for IBM and compatible machines, and is also available for multi user work on a Xenix network.

NewsWriter represents an excellent program for general office use, as well as for creative writers, who do not want to be bothered with the complexities of page layout.

The second non–WYSIWYG program, although it does have a 'page preview' option, is only available for the Apple Macintosh. It is called 'JustText' and is very like traditional typesetting software in that it is command driven.

JustText

JustText is a very powerful wordprocessor, like NewsWriter, but does not allow the user to be totally free of decisions about layout, fount selection and so on. All of the information regarding the width and positioning of columns on the page, the typeface, size and so on, has to be entered using command codes (see Figure 9). Although this sounds complicated, it is comparatively easy, especially for anyone who has ever used command driven programs which is ironically unlikely for anyone who has always used a Macintosh! However, using the JustText codes does allow for more precise control over page layouts than is possible with some of the other page make—up software.

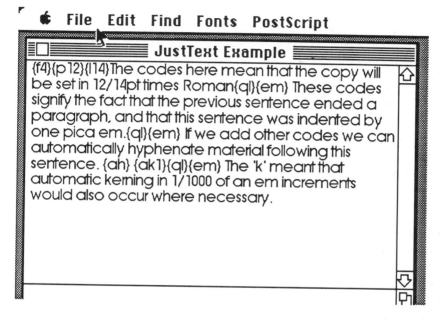

Figure 9 — An example of JustText coded writing as it might appear on the Macintosh screen

The real power with JustText is that you can work directly in PostScript, the industry standard page description language for laser printers, which can also be understood by Linotronic typesetters. JustText, therefore, allows competent users to perform layout and textual tricks unavailable in many other page make—up programs. Also, since JustText allows users to write programs in PostScript, it means that the application can be used with *any* PostScript compatible devices, such as the Linotronic 100 or Linotronic 300 typesetting machines.

JustText is a very powerful program. It supports all of the usual desktop publishing requirements of hyphenation and justification. Because of PostScript's ability to define precise movements on the page it is possible to write in short pieces of program codes for graphics. JustText can also import graphics from drawing programs used on the Macintosh.

Because of the sheer power of JustText it is unlikely to find a home in the general office environment. It is, though, very useful for workers in the traditional publishing industry breaking in to the desktop publishing world, as well as for creative workers, such as people in advertising and design. It is also likely to be very useful for typesetting firms wishing to provide desktop publishing facilities for customers who do not have computers. Traditional typesetting keyboard operators will not find the JustText program very much different to the command driven world they already live in. However, the use of some of the other desktop publishing programs by such keyboard operators may need more retraining.

Other than JustText and NewsWriter, the world of non–WYSIWYG page make–up programs is surprisingly slim. There are, of course, sophisticated wordprocessing packages available, which can produce attractive laser printer output but do not offer the full range of desktop publishing facilities, such as the inclusion of graphics.

Some of these programs do have WYSIWYG; others do not, especially if they are using a non–enhanced IBM type machine. Such wordprocessors, which support multi–columns and a range of founts may be perfectly acceptable for many office–based publishing projects. However, they are not flexible enough for many of the top end publishing projects, such as magazine design etc. For this sort of publishing and for many other areas, including manuals, books and annual reports, only the true WYSIWYG page make–up programs will provide some users with what they want — unless they have opted for NewsWriter or JustText instead.

PageMaker

The first true page make–up program to become widely available is a program called PageMaker. It was initially only available for the Apple Macintosh, but is now also available for IBM and compatible machines, and is likely to become available for other computers, such as Wang. It is still the program against which all others are compared, is in widespread use and has, therefore, a lot of experienced users.

PageMaker is the one program, out of a constantly growing number, which works most like a traditional publishing environment.

PageMaker places material on a page in exactly the same way as a magazine sub–editor might do, as described in the previous chapter.

PageMaker allows you to import wordprocessed material from a wordprocessor; in the case of the Macintosh MacWrite, Microsoft Works, or Microsoft Word; and in the case of IBM,all of the major programs such as Wordstar, Word Perfect, Microsoft Word etc. All of the formats entered into the wordprocessor files are carried over into PageMaker, where they can be accepted, or altered. You can also import graphics material from programs such as MacDraw, MacDraft, MacPaint, and Cricket Graph, for the Macintosh, and PC Paint, AutoCAD, Lotus 123 and Symphony (to name just a few) for the IBM PC. Both the IBM and the Macintosh versions of PageMaker allow you to import PostScript commands directly to perform fancy effects and textual tricks.

When you start a publication in PageMaker you choose the size of the paper you want (this can be selected from a range of standard sizes including A4 and American Legal, or defined by the user) and specify the number of pages — up to 128. You can then define standard items on master pages, such as numbers of columns, rules and page numbering. You need not define these particulars for the entire publication, though they can be done for each individual page. This is especially handy if you want to have a different number of columns on each page.

Once your basics are sorted out you can begin to add material to the pages from wordprocessor files and graphics files. These are imported using the 'place' command. You select a file to be placed on the page and then point to the position on the page where you want the material to appear. Instantly the file appears there. If it is a text file it runs down the column until all of the text has been placed, or until it reaches a barrier, such as the bottom of the column, a previously placed piece of text, or a graphic. The bottom of the newly placed text then has a cross at the bottom of it indicating that more text still has to be placed. By clicking the pointer of the mouse on this cross, then clicking where you want the text to continue the remaining copy is 'picked up' by the mouse pointer and run down the column. This is the essential difference between PageMaker and other desktop publishing programs.

PageMaker does not automatically flow copy from one column to the next, as some other programs can do. It stops flowing text when it reaches a barrier allowing the operator to decide where the text should continue. PageMaker therefore provides desktop publishers with the same sort of flexibility as a compositor has in a typesetting house. Some other programs need careful setting up to provide the same degree of flexibility. For people who wish to run large amounts of text from one column to the next throughout a long publication PageMaker can be a bit if a bind since you have to place each column independently.

However, for publications such as magazines, newspapers, and newsletters where the design is complex and material does not necessarily flow from one column to the top of the next one PageMaker is an ideal program. Out of all of the available desktop publishing software it is the one which most resembles the world of newspaper and magazine publishing layout. It is therefore of particular value to people performing such tasks.

PageMaker is a very powerful program with all of the usual desktop publishing requirements such as hyphenation. It also has a good text editor which allows you to enter text directly rather than import it from a wordprocessor file. But it does not have the powerful aspects of wordprocessors, such as search and replace. It is worthwhile remembering that software is continually upgraded so it seems likely that this feature will be added, as will automatic text flow for people who require it. Another feature which is expected to be added to PageMaker is called 'runaround'. This is the ability to run text around a graphic (see Figure 10) without having to play around altering the column width. If you decide to move the graphic the text automatically adjusts itself around it, so that no white space or overlap occurs. This is a very useful and time–saving feature, which is already included in another leading page make–up program called Ventura Publisher.

Ventura

Ventura is probably going to be the biggest single competitor to PageMaker in the IBM market. Ventura is only available for IBM machines and compatibles, and is a product available from the originators of desktop publishing, Rank Xerox.

Ventura has all of the usual desktop publishing requirements, such as hyphenation, justification, and fount selection. It is a true WYSIWYG program and supports publications with unlimited numbers of pages. You can, just like PageMaker, control the leading, column widths etc, that you can have a good typographical

Text which is said to run around graphics does just that. It goes around the shape of the graphic leaving space wherever necessary so that the graphic can be seen. If the graphic image is moved, programs require the operator to make the vital decisions, rather there is extra time taken up with moving the text around the graphics. This does not happen with the automatic programs But it's true that doing it manually

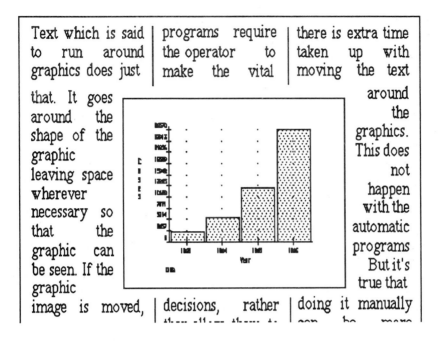

Figure 10 — An example of what is meant by running text around a graphic

appearance but the basic way of operating Ventura is different to PageMaker.

Ventura has 'style sheets'. These are basic styles for pages, parts of pages, whole publications, and so on. The choice is yours. Each style sheet can contain specified columns, typefaces and sizes. All you need to do is tell the program which wordprocessor or graphics file you want to place in the page or document. Ventura then places it in the document, automatically hyphenating and justifying if requested, until all of the file is in position. It also does this remarkably fast. Ventura is ideal for the production of standard documents and is very useful in an office publishing environment, where there is a requirement for a wide range of standard documents, such as brochures, sales leaflets, annual reports etc.

Ventura also allows individual page control. You specify an area of the page which will accept graphics and an area for text. You can manipulate these areas if you wish until they are in the right position, then import material from other files into the correct place. In this respect it is similar to PageMaker, although with PageMaker you do not have to go through the process of telling the program which areas are for graphics or text. PageMaker does not need to have pre-defined poritions of the page; you can put text or graphics anywhere you like. With Ventura you can put text or graphics anywhere you like but you must first define both text and graphics areas. This, therefore, adds a stage to the design function and may prove frustrating in the publication of newsletters etc which have different designs with every edition. But by the use of style sheets, Ventura can be used by people with less experience of design and page layout, since all of this work can be done by an experienced operator prior to work beginning.

For example with Ventura an experienced designer can set up a number of style sheets for such things as a staff newsletter, a manual, a book, a proposal and a brochure. All that the less experienced operators need to do is to select the text or graphics required for the publication they are working on, then place it in a copy of the appropriate style sheet.

The only disadvantage to this quite simple scheme of things, is that it can lead to repetition of layouts, thus increasing similarity between publications. This similarity can be responsible for confusion amongst readers and may, therefore, contribute to reductions in readership levels for something like a newsletter. If the newsletter has identical layouts for each and every issue readers will become confused as to which issue they are looking at. They may think they have already read it. For newsletters Ventura requires a more experienced operator, who can change design rather than use pre-formatted style sheets. Experienced newspaper and magazine designers may find that the pre–defining of text and graphic areas is a little frustrating, and may therefore prefer PageMaker. However, for office publishing there is little to choose between the two packages. It is interesting to note that PageMaker is now sold bundled with the Apricot IBM compatible Xen computers. Ventura is sold only as an off–the–shelf program by Rank Xerox licensed distributors and dealers.

Documentor

Rank Xerox has retained another of its developments called 'Documentor', a bundle of software and IBM compatible hardware.

Documentor is aimed virtually exclusively at office–based publishing operations.

The program includes a special forms generator not included with either Ventura or PageMaker, although, obviously, you can construct forms with these programs. Documentor is a package — program, computer, and laser printer. Unlike the Apple Macintosh the Documentor has a large screen which is true WYSIWYG.

The Documentor package appears to be most suited to office publishing where not too much creative expertise is available. It is an easy to use system, can work on a network and will also support colour laser writers. Colour laser writers are expected for early 1988 and Documentor and Ventura are already able to cope with this development. However, the advent of colour laser writers is probably not worth worrying about. As already explained, the most useful aspect of laser writers is their ability to produce CRC. This only ever needs to be produced in black and white. Colour laser writers are likely to be very expensive and, whilst the addition of colour to low circulation publications printed directly by a laser printer could be an advantage, the cost will need to be carefully considered. But if you do want to use a colour laser printer Documentor software will allow you to do so without needing to upgrade the program contained in the package.

The only possible sticking point with Documentor is the fact that it does not support PostScript. Instead it supports another page description language called 'Interpress'.

This can be understood by Compugraphic typesetting machines, but the widespread influence of PostScript may mean that it is more difficult to find a typesetter who will print out Interpress based material. For those people who do want a PostScript system, and for whom something like the Documentor forms generator is important, a new product from Canada may be worth looking at. This is called 'The Office Publisher' from a company called 'Laser Friendly'.

Office Publisher

The Office Publisher is an IBM compatible program, which has a forms generator as well as being a powerful page make–up application. A more powerful version called 'Office Publisher Plus' is also available. The packages have a variety of pre-designed pages for such things as directories, price lists, brochures etc. Whilst these may be very useful for inexperienced users of desktop publishing software and may be extremely useful in office publishing situations, it may contribute to a degree of 'sameness' of publications. As already mentioned this could be off–putting to readers and purchasers may find themselves abandoning the pre–formated designs and producing their own. Presumably the pre–formated designs have only been included as a guide to help inexperienced operators. This is something which can be of help to companies, who have little or no experience of desktop publishing. Training is expensive and experienced designers may need to be recruited to co-ordinate office publishing activities. Consequently the use of pre–formated pages can be helpful in learning how to use the software. But try to avoid using such pages too often since you may find yourself producing a range of documents which appear very similar. It can become too convenient to opt for the 'easy way out' by using pre–formatted designs, such as those included in The Office Publisher. (Other programs, such as Ventura, also include these helpful basic page layouts).

The Office Publisher Plus allows complete control over typography and design and is certainly the better of the two from Laser Friendly for companies who will have a greater demand for publishing facilities other than well–presented documents (adequately coped with by The Office Publisher).

Page Designer Systems

Page Designer Systems is a suite of software for MS-DOS and PC-DOS computers aimed squarely at the office publishing market. The most basic of the Page Designer Systems programs is called FDP — Forms Design Package. This is a very flexible and easy to use program, which could be used at secretarial level, if necessary, to design all manner of forms, flyers, leaflets, notices, direct mail shots, overhead transparency slides, etc. If your office publishing needs extend no further than these simple requirements, then FDP is well worth looking at. However, FDP is only the most basic of the Page Designer Systems suite. The other programs in this group of software will be able to incorporate graphics, design founts and so on, as well has having a useful library of symbols. The suite of software also operates with a wide range of laser printers, such as those made by Canon and Hewlett Packard, two of the leading manufacturers.

Canon Personal Publishing System

An alternative option for office based publishing is the Canon Personal Publishing System. Like Documentor this is a package, including an IBM compatible computer, the necessary software and a laser printer. Like Documentor and The Office Publisher the Canon system has a forms generator.

The software with this package is suited to uncomplicated office publishing needs rather than to the production of complex design magazines and newsletters.

JetSetter

Another possible office publishing system is one called JetSetter. This has the usual desktop publishing functions such as fount selection and so on. This is an excellent program, since it is very easy to use and quick to learn. It has only one menu from which an operator chooses founts, column widths, justification etc. You toggle between the menu page and the work page using a control key. The software does not need a mouse but will work with one if you prefer. JetSetter is for the HP Vectra computer, IBM PC-ATs and compatibles. The program requires, quite logically, as will be explained later, that text is prepared in a wordprocessor, then placed on the page. JetSetter can also accept graphics from the Lotus standard.

In terms of selection, the JetSetter program does appear at first sight rather limited. There are only three typefaces, for example, Times, Helvetica, and Souvenir (this is one of the only programs to offer Souvenir as standard, which is interesting since this typeface is one of the most widely used display types in traditional publishing).

The program also only allows you to work on one page at a time. When compared to PageMaker this may seem rather poor. However, JetSetter is not meant to be an imitator of PageMaker. PageMaker would almost certainly be a daunting prospect for newcomers to publishing, whereas JetSetter is unlikely to face the same problem.

JetSetter does have fewer options than PageMaker The choices which PageMaker offers are excellent for experienced page layout designers but for people new to publishing the variety of options available can help lead to some pretty ugly layouts because of overuse, or misuse of the variations. With the constraints of JetSetter, novice office publishers could well be able to produce more attractive looking publications because they cannot play about with too many features! JetSetter is an ideal program for use by secretaries, or managers themselves who only have a rudimentary knowledge of keyboard operation.

Protex

Another package to be considered is one called Protex. Protex has all of the usual desktop publishing requirements — hyphenation, justification etc. It also has a spelling checker and is a powerful wordprocessor. It is an IBM PC or compatible program and can run on networks too. But it is limited in terms of standard fount selection.

Fleet Street Editor

A further option to consider is one called Fleet Street Editor, not to be confused with Fleet Street Editor, or Fleet Street Editor! Unfortunately Mirrorsoft, the software arm of Mirror Group Publishing, has brought out a number of programs, all called Fleet Street Editor. Whilst they are all basically the same, there are differences between them, according to the type of hardware they run upon. For example, there is a Fleet Street Editor for the Amstrad CPC series and the BBC B or Acorn Master computer, and also a Fleet Street Editor for the IBM PC and compatibles. The IBM PC version is the most powerful of the bunch and will do much of the basic requirements of desktop publishing. Because it is a powerful program, and fairly inexpensive, it is ideal for use on low cost computers such as the Amstrad PC1512 IBM compatibles.

Anyone who wishes to use a highly professional desktop publishing program, such as PageMaker, but cannot afford it, could look at a newer program from Mirrorsoft called Fleet Street Publisher 2. This does all of the sorts of things which PageMaker does, supports PostScript devices as well as other typesetting machines, and accepts text and graphics from a variety of other programs.

Fleet Street Publisher

Fleet Street Publisher works on the Atari 1040ST and, therefore, offers an economic alternative to many packages. However, Fleet Street Publisher cannot be used on a network, although the less powerful Fleet Street Editor will work on an IBM network.

For people who do not have an IBM PC or compatible and own an Apple Macintosh there is a wide choice of software. PageMaker is the Rolls Royce of Macintosh software, but there are other powerful programs available. The largest competitor to PageMaker in the Macintosh market is called Ready Set Go 3, or RSG3.

Ready Set Go 3

RSG3 is very much like Ventura. You can create basic styles and pre-define areas of text and graphics before any material is imported onto a page. Text automatically reflows from one column to the next, provided you have selected the column linkage option. This clever little device means that you can, for example, make text flow automatically from column one on the first page to column four on page 12, if you needed to. This device is likely to be of real use in magazine work where long articles are often carried over to later pages.

A slight problem with RSG3 is in the placing of graphics. With PageMaker you can leave a space for graphics to be placed at a printer. This may be necessary when using photographs, or when adding four colour material. With RSG3, when graphics are embedded within text you need to specify a graphics ares, just as you would with Ventura. If you do not place any graphics in the area, as you would not do if these were to be added at the printing stage for technical reasons, RSG3 prints out the graphics area as a box with a cross in it. This may be very useful for proof pages but will be troublesome if you are producing CRC! The answer is to enter a simple box into the graphics area. This need only be a half point 'keyline' which will border the picture when it is inserted by the printers onto the plates. By not doing this you could end up with a cross in the middle of your picture! It is only a little annoying problem but it is one which is completely avoided by PageMaker, which does not require the page to be broken up into text or graphics areas.

Another annoying problem with RSG3 is that if you are working in large documents (the number of pages is limited only by computer memory) it is difficult to make quick changes to the master pages. At the bottom left of the screen there are a number of icons which represent the pages in the document. You can go direct to a page by clicking on its icon. When you scroll through a long document the early pages disappear off the left of the screen as the later pages come in from the right.

The first two pages are the master pages. If you want to change these you have to scroll back through the page icons until you get to them! With PageMaker the master page icons are always present on the screen, with the actual page icons scrolling behind them. This means you can make master page changes more easily with PageMaker than with RSG3. It is only a very minor problem but may annoy some people. Nevertheless, RSG 3 is a very able and comprehensive program and very competitively priced against PageMaker. It could become a serious contender against PageMaker for the Macintosh.

Ragtime

This Macintosh system is unusual and a real 'first' in terms of desktop publishing software. 'Ragtime' is the first integrated package, which incorporates a page layout program. The rest of the package is a wordprocessor, a forms generator and graphics manager, together with a spreadsheet. This package may prove to be one of the most useful for company reports where financial or statistical information prepared in spreadsheet format needs to be put together in an attractive publication.

Ragtime is less comprehensive in terms of page layout when compared to PageMaker, but if your desktop publishing demands are less complex and will regularly involve spreadsheet information the integration provided by Ragtime is likely to be more useful than having to cut and paste material, opening and closing applications with something like PageMaker.

Other Programs

There are of course other page layout programs for the Mac and for IBM computers and compatibles. These include MacAuthor, an excellent wordprocessor and basic page layout system, Graphic Works and TeX, all for the Apple Macintosh. Then there is Harvard Professional Publisher, Deskset, Front Page and Xtraset for IBMs and compatibles. All of these and many others have their advantages and disadvantages, and should be investigated if you are looking for the package which suits you best. Details of where to obtain information can be found in Chapter 8.

There are some basic things which should be remembered in the hunt for good desktop publishing software. Firstly, no one program is likely to do everything you want it to do and you may well have to buy two programs to be able to cope with all of your various publishing needs. Secondly, PageMaker is the industry standard against which all others are measured. It is widely available on the Apple Macintosh, is being increasingly used on the IBM PC and compatibles, and soon to become available for both Wang and DEC machines. This shows that PageMaker is regarded as the most influential desktop publishing program around.

For the IBM market, especially in the office publishing arena, it looks like PageMaker will be competing heavily against Ventura, which is more easily used by less experienced operators. NewsWriter and JetSetter will both play a significant part in office publishing if secretaries are asked to produce office publications quickly and easily.

But whatever software you choose, you will then be able to decide upon the hardware. If your software choice is limited by already existing hardware then you will be spared the necessity of having to decide between a Macintosh or an IBM if you have settled upon PageMaker! A useful point to remember is that PageMaker was originally designed to run on the Macintosh, that the Macintosh is a natural WIMP environment and does not need the additional help of Microsoft Windows or GEM and, as already mentioned, PageMaker is the truest representation of what a newspaper or magazine designer does on paper.

The Macintosh is amongst the favourite pieces of hardware for professionals in the world of publishing and can be seen in many magazine and newspaper offices. If your demands are for good desktop publishing using PageMaker, then the Apple Macintosh may prove to be the ideal choice. If you already have an IBM style machine and you want creative flexibility, then PageMaker running under the WIMP environment of Microsoft Windows may also prove to be a good choice.

However, some people may wish to have the user friendliness of NewsWriter, which means you are limited in your choice of hardware. Ventura, too, will limit you to IBM and compatibles. Documentor software is only available as a package with the hardware. Ragtime only runs on the Mac. And so on.

Some people will want technical ability and mathematical languages for desktop publishing. These are not present in the vast majority of desktop publishing packages but one worth looking at is called Soft Quad for UNIX systems. Another which can be used on the Apple Macintosh with MacAuthor is called MacEqn. Other dedicated technical page make–up programs are expected to become available during 1987.

For general desktop publishing needs, it is important to remember that PageMaker will run on the vast majority of computers in current use — IBM PCs and compatibles. Until programs like Ventura, Ready Set Go 3, NewsWriter, or JetSetter take a greater hold in the market desktop publishing seems very likely to be dominated by PageMaker. However, if the flexibility and power of PageMaker is too much for your needs there are plenty of suitable programs, with more being developed virtually daily.

Fortunately these programs are available for most hardware options. Choose your program and then worry about the hardware you want afterwards!

Laser Printers

Once you have chosen your basic hardware, which will cope with your chosen software, has at least 512k RAM, a paper white screen, a hard disk, etc., you will then be able to decide on a laser printer. The laser printers in the most common use already are those manufactured by Hewlett Packard — the LaserJet range of printers. These printers use a 'document description language' (DDL) rather than the PDL PostScript. DDL is reckoned to be slightly faster than PostScript, although, as already stated, this is not really something which requires a great deal of discussion or worry in practical terms. PostScript describes individual pages, whereas DDL describes a whole *document*, hence the name.

Existing LaserJet printers can be upgraded to understand the language and programs like PageMaker will be able to drive the printers with the addition of software updates. But DDL cannot be understood by Linotronic typesetting machines so it can limit anyone who wishes to improve quality by taking disks to typesetters for running off through such a machine.

The other main player in laser printers is the Apple LaserWriter. This is a 300 dpi PostScript machine and can therefore be linked to any computer which will send out PostScript. It is one of the more expensive laser printers available. However, it does seem likely that higher resolution printers will become available.

Agfa have a 400 dots per inch (dpi) laser printer available. Although this does not sound much of an improvement over 300 dpi of most laser printers it is in fact quite large. A 300 dpi printer produces only 90,000 dots in each square inch. Whereas the Agfa printer produces 160,000 dots per square inch, an improvement of more than 75 per cent.

If you need to print pages larger than A4 or American legal, one option is the Data Products A3 printer. This prints out at twice the size of most laser printers and at a faster rate of pages per minute. But it is much more expensive. If you really desparately do need A3 artwork this may well be the only option.

There are other A3 laser printers available, but they are expensive and can cost more than double the Data Products machine which is already almost twice the price of an Apple LaserWriter! For most people though A4 is sufficient and the range of printers is quite wide.

Laser Master, for example, has a wide range of laser printers. Kyocera is a Japanese firm which produces laser printers. These printers can emulate a number of different printers such as LaserJets, IBM printers, Diablo, Epson etc. They can also print out bar codes, useful if your publication is to have an International Standard Book Number (ISBN) or an International Standard Serial Number (ISSN).

If you buy Documentor, the Xerox laser printer you get with the package also doubles as a photocopier. This may be very useful for small businesses where capital expenditure needs to be controlled, or for departments not close to central photocopying facilities.

When choosing a laser printer there are a few things to check. Will it be able to print material produced by your software? Does it have a high enough resolution? Some IBM printers, for example, are at only 240 dpi — around 30 per cent fewer dots per square inch compared to 300 dpi machines. How many pages will the toner print and at what cost? How long is the engine expected to last at maximum use? Does it support PostScript if you need it? Only by answering these questions will you be able to find the printer most suited to your needs. At a rough guess this will mean either Hewlett Packard, Apple, or Canon, since these are the three leading makes in current use. New printers and enhancements are being developed every week, so check with a number of dealers. You should also remember that not every laser printer supports a wide range of founts. For some printers you have to load founts from a cartridge, whereas others can have founts downloaded from a disk. If a wide range of founts is necessary choose your printer with care after having made the dealer show you the machine actually printing out a number of different founts!

Hardware Extras

Once you have settled upon a program, a computer and a laser printer, you are still left with the possibility of choosing hardware add—ons to help with desktop publishing. A very useful one is a modem, so that you can obtain information from databases and incorporate it into your publications (be wary of copyright — see Chapter 7). More importantly though, a modem will be useful to obtain copy from 'reporters' and other contributors. It will also allow you to send files to some typesetting bureaux for passing through a typesetting machine.

The other main desktop publishing optional piece of hardware is a 'scanner' or 'digitiser'. This is a device which converts a graphic or a photograph into a digital information which can be interpreted by a computer. There are two basic types. One relies on placing the material in front of a video camera, which literally records the information for the computer. The alternative is similar to a photocopier, in that you place the material to be incorporated into your computer—based documents on a glass screen. The picture is scanned and converted into digital information. Another type of digitiser actually rolls the material to be transferred to the computer through a printer—like machine. Macintosh users can even convert their ImageWriter printers to do a similar job with a product called Thunderscan.

Scanners like these convert the image into dot for dot information. Most work on a 300dpi basis. This means that photographs, for example, can be printed out on a laser printer. But as already explained, laser printers are low in resolution compared to traditional origination methods. Consequently, scanned images from photographs can look very poor. This problem will be overcome with the introduction of higher resolution laser printers and scanning machines. If you want to place photographs within desktop publications, the easiest way for good quality is to have the photographs 'stripped–in' by a printer at the printing stage.

The printer will screen the photographs at a much higher effective resolution thus providing better quality. This will increase printing bills slightly but will avoid spending cash on relatively expensive digitisers. Such machines though, are invaluable in transferring line drawings to computer based publications since they avoid the necessity of drawing the graphics all over again. Once incorporated into a document, page make–up programs allow these graphics, like all others, to be manipulated easily. However, some page make–up programs do not allow the direct import of scanned material. They have to be scanned into a draw program first, then transferred from there. If you will require a scanner and expect to use it frequently, be sure that the page make–up program you want will accept scanned images directly. If this is not the case, you could spend a bit of time transferring the image to and from a draw program, which will not take as long as redrawing the graphic from scratch but will be mildly annoying.

Once you have got all of your desktop publishing package ordered, you will need to think about where it is to go, who will be the first to receive training, how you will arrange hardware and software security, etc. All of these topics have been covered widely in a range of publications. Suffice it to say that desktop publishing is an expensive business in terms of office computing. Many people will want the laser printer because it makes their letters look better than a daisy–wheel or dot–matrix. Before long your laser printer will be on a network providing printed output for everyone! That will considerably reduce the amount of time the publishing operation has on the machine and will also reduce its lifespan, thus increasing capital costs.

Health Risks

One other point about desktop publishing packages. There has been some discussion about the supposed health risks of laser printers. They are based on photocopying technology and there have been claims that some of these are hazardous to health. Fortunately, there appears to be no truth in the accusations. The laser is completely enclosed and the potential problems of some toner inks, which were identified many years ago, have been avoided by changing the constituents of the inks used. The only real health hazard with desktop publishing is that of general computer use.

Backache, neckache and eyestrain are common complaints of people who use computers. They are nothing whatsoever to do with the computers but rather the way in which we use them. We have our chairs at the wrong heights, our desks are also poorly positioned and we don't seem to take breaks from looking at the screen, thus making our eyes perform extra work by continually focusing.

To avoid these problems never sit working at a computer for more than 50 minutes in every hour; have a fully adjustable chair which has a moveable back support. When sitting your feet should be flat on the floor and your knees at right angles with your thighs parallel to the floor. Your arms should be at right angles at the elbow with your forearms parallel to the floor when typing at the keyboard. If you take note of these simple tips you should be able to spend many happy hours editing and producing desktop publications.

Chapter 5

Planning for Desktop Publishing

No journalist ever writes an article without planning what to say; no author ever writes a book without outlining each chapter; and no businessman ever operates a company without planning its strategy and operation. So why oh why do so many publications appear to be so unplanned!

If you take a look at publications like some in-house magazines, some sales brochures, small circulation newsletters, and commercial magazines that have failed, you will notice a common theme. The obvious lack of any kind of planning to identify an audience and provide it with well written, interesting and clearly laid out material.

Research and practical experience has shown many publishers that planning is essential, both in terms of identifying a market and serving it. If planning for publishing is a shoddy affair, or one which is neglected, or given too little time, the end result is a publication which has no clearly defined target audience. The content has no common theme, and is laid out so appallingly, that many people who do venture into the pages of the publication become confused and, consequently, give up reading any further.

Planning any kind of publication must be within the framework of the publishing process, already outlined in Chapter 3. The fact that you will be using desktop publishing technology and not the slow, laborious and expensive methods of traditional publishing does not lead to any real differences in terms of planning. The publication is the key, not the method by which it is produced.

So you have an idea for a publication. Do you know who will read it? Can you clearly define an audience? If you cannot clearly specify a group of people who will be interested in reading the proposed publication, then think again. No one is going to be interested in a publication which applies to too wide an audience.

For example, a company may be thinking of setting up a publication on the activities of the firm. Now whilst the staff may be interested to read about the activities of colleagues in other departments, offices, or factories, this 'gossip' will be of little interest to shareholders, who are far more interested in the company's export potential, or its improvements in handling distribution. No doubt some members of staff would also be interested in hearing some of this sort of information but not necessarily in the depth required by shareholders. A further group of people who could be interested in information on the company would be existing customers. Potential customers may also be willing to read about the activities of the firm. So there are four possible audiences — staff, shareholders, customers and potential customers.

To produce one publication on the activities of a company, which would satisfy these four diverse audiences, would be possible but not advisable. The differing reading interests of the audiences would make the publication's content so wide–ranging that each group would be able to spot more articles of no real interest, than they could identify as absorbing. The result would be that few people would bother to read the publication at all, and the company's money would be wasted, since the newsletter would clearly not be an efficient way of communicating.

A far better method for producing efficient communications in this example would be to have four newsletters — one for each individual group. Each newsletter would contain articles of interest only to the particular readership. However, there may be a few articles which would be of interest to more than one readership grouping. Thanks to desktop publishing technology, you would be able to copy articles, or whole pages, from one newsletter to another. If you were to do this, then you should ensure there is a common design theme running through all the publications, otherwise copies of articles and pages will stick out plainly as being something different.

Deciding on your audience, the first stage of planning, is also important in other areas of publishing, say in the production of sales leaflets. For example, if your company produces a wide–range of products for various markets it would be of little help to have all of your products covered in one leaflet. Some of the products listed would be of no interest to certain readers. You would have given them useless information. With traditional publishing methods most companies appear to have followed the simple marketing rule of hitting your target audience with exactly what they want, or think they want. However, with the advent of desktop publishing and the ability to produce such sales literature in–house, there does appear, in some cases, to have been a change in this way of thinking. Companies producing their own sales literature seem to have been taken over by the technology and its ability to manipulate text and graphics. The result has been sales material which is covered with everything! This shows a simple lack of planning for a specific target audience.

The rule should be quite obvious. Whatever kind of publication you intend producing, make sure that it is being put together for a clearly defined target audience. If you do not do this you will lose readers and stop gaining readers as well. The result will be a failed publication, or an expensive company experiment, which did not effectively communicate.

Once you have defined your target audience, decided on what sort of articles this audience would like to read, made up your mind about whether or not to accept advertising and followed all of the steps suggested in Chapter 3, you will be ready to actually plan your publication.The first step in planning will be in deciding the size, format, and 'pagination' of the item. Pagination is the publishers' shorthand for saying 'the number of pages in the publication'. You will then need to consider the quality of paper, method of printing, number of copies, method of distribution and so on. Do not start producing your publication until you know how it will be printed, by whom, how much this will cost and how long it will take; how the publication will be distributed and at what cost; how long distribution will take. As suggested in Chapter 3 all of these questions need answering prior to any work beginning on the publication.

Printing options are covered in Chapter 3. The best method is to use a laser printer to produce master pages of 'Camera Ready Copy' (CRC), which a commercial printer can then use to run off as many copies of your publication as required. Only use a laser printer for the actual printing of a fairly small run of copies, around less than 100. This will extend the life of your laser printer but no doubt upset your computer dealer. The dealer hopes that you will use the machine frequently, for a lot of pages, so that you have to be kept supplied with toner and hopefully, within three years, a spanking new printing 'engine'!

Distribution is more problematic than anything else. Getting your publication printed, even in four colour, is easy when compared to the difficulties of distribution.If you do have a publication which is likely to sell in hundreds of thousands, then distribution through a wholesaler to newsagents is cost effective. But for small run magazines and newsletters there are other ways of distribution which should be considered. These include house to house delivery, direct mailing, 'bulk dropping' and mail order. All of these have their advantages and disadvantages, which will be considered in Chapter 7. In the meantime, it is important to remember to choose a method of distribution when planning a publication and set it up, before you start work on the publication itself.

With all of this basic, but essential, work done you should be able to deal with editorial planning. As already described in Chapter 3, editorial planning is vital if your publication is to be produced on time with the minimum of trouble, and so that you put together a publication which is of real interest to your target readership. Such planning will depend upon the exact type of publication you intend producing, so we shall now look at some specific examples.

Newsletters

Desktop publishing has meant that many more newsletters are being produced than before. In the past newsletter publication was either expensive if traditional publishing techniques were employed, or the results were not very professional since they were simply copies of typewritten material.

Now desktop publishing has made the whole process of producing professional looking newsletters very much easier. Indeed one company, the Financial Times in London, has a newsletter division — the largest newsletter publishers in Europe — which use the desktop publishing program 'NewsWriter' to put its publications together.

There are basically two types of newsletter but both have a relatively low circulation to a clearly defined target audience. The first type of newsletter is that distributed to members of a club or society, for example. The second type is the commercial newsletter bought for large sums of money, usually more than £10 ($15) an issue, because of the high level content.

Both types of newsletters have one thing in common. They are geared to a small readership, who cannot obtain the information elsewhere, or if they can, only with difficulty. Some newsletters will therefore contain original information which is virtually exclusive, or they may be 'digests' of information culled from a variety of sources. This digest type newsletter provides readers with an update on the subject matter, thus preventing them having to spend hours wading through a variety of different publications.

The first stage of newsletter planning is to decide which type of newsletter it shall be. Is it going to contain exclusive information, or will it be a digest? If it is to contain highly original material, who will provide it? If it is to be a digest, where will the information come from? Sort out the answers to these questions first, before proceeding to the next stage — overall design.

Newsletter design appears to have been a largely forgotten aspect of publishing, if some of the examples of desktop published newsletters are to be believed! The first thing to consider is the overall look you are trying to achieve. Do you want the newsletter to look sombre and heavyweight or fun? Do you want it to look considered and thoughtful, or do you want it to look full of information and busy? The overall style you want for the publication will, in some way, limit your design choices. For example, a serious, thought provoking article would look out of place in a bright, brash, tabloid newspaper style newsletter.

Once you have given some thought to the overall style and the 'look' you are trying to achieve, then you need to plan the overall layout constraints. This will be rather like the house style guide mentioned in Chapter 3. Indeed many publishers include the basic design as part of the house style book. The first layout constraint to be considered is the number of columns. Most newsletters are published on A4, and the maximum number of columns which can be considered is four. A greater number than this will lead to too many word breaks, since the columns will be narrow, which only increases the difficulty of reading. A few basic newsletter layout grids are shown in the Appendix.

You should also be wary of using only one column. Research has shown columns which are too wide can also increase reading difficulty. If you do use wide columns you must have a higher type size than you could use on a column of narrower width. Two or three columns is the best idea for an A4 newsletter, with three columns being the ideal choice, since this allows a greater flexibility when designing individual pages.

A three column A4 page could have columns which are 15 pica ems wide with a one pica em gutter running between them. A two column page could have columns of 20 pica ems, with a gutter of one pica em. Some newsletters have unequal column widths. This is usually the case when the narrower left–hand column has 'headlines' and sub–headings in it, with the wider right–hand column containing the text. This sort of layout is a very sober type of design and only really suitable for newsletters containing important and original information for commercial organisations.

Having decided on your basic layout constraints of columns, gutters etc., you now produce a 'grid', a blank page which contains faint lines representing the outer edges of your columns. This can be achieved with most of the desktop publishing software available, although you may need to draw a box to represent the columns once you have set up a master page. Desktop publishing at its best offers true WYSIWYG but for people using an Apple Macintosh without an add—on large screen, and certainly for beginners to the world of Desktop Publishing, the screen does not seem to show you exactly how a page will look. The screen really does show you what the page will look like but can take some getting used to if you normally work on paper. In the early stages of your desktop publishing experiences a basic grid will be a help in planning your design. Traditional publishing houses have pre—printed grids for all of their publications. These are used by the sub—editors to draw page layouts upon. The equivalent in desktop publishing are the master pages of programs like PageMaker, or the style sheets of something such as Ventura. If you are entering desktop publishing for the first time print out a basic grid just to give you a feel of the page and its columns. After you have been using desktop publishing technology for a while you should find this unnecessary.

With the grid in front of you and a special ruler called an 'em rule', you will be able to go on to the next stage of design. An em rule not only has inches and centimetres upon it but is also graduated in pica ems and pica 'ens' (half an em), as well as perhaps in other measurements, such as 10pt units, or 5pt units.

Em rules can be found at good drawing shops and in some office stationers. If in doubt, contact a local publisher or a typesetter and ask where they buy their em rules. Even in desktop publishing an em rule is invaluable, despite the fact that most programs allow you to place a simple em rule up on the screen. You will, for example, need an em rule when dealing with photographs.

With your em rule and your basic grid you will be able to mark off depths in a column for such things as headlines, or even graphics. By quickly drawing a rough page with these tools you will be able to see what sort of size headlines and so on your page will require. A general rule to remember is that the more serious and sober you want your newsletter to look, the smaller the size of display type used in headlines.

Having played around with your grid you should be able to work on the screen to start producing the results you want. You should not avoid working on paper to begin with since it will help you clarify in your mind how high 72pt looks on an A4 page. Although the screen will show you 72pt exactly, it is difficult to visualise this on paper, unless you are already well—versed in publication production.

With the number of columns decided and having used a grid and an em rule to gain some idea about how you want your publication to look, you should then decide upon the typefaces. As already mentioned, no page of A4 should contain more than three typefaces.

If a page does have a large collection of faces it looks too busy, more like an explosion in a typesetting factory than a professionally produced publication. Your choice of typeface will be limited by the typefaces supported by your printer. For some laser printers there are only a handful of typefaces. For others, like the Apple LaserWriter, the number of typefaces is virtually limitless since you can 'download' individual faces into the RAM of the computer on board the printer. There are even typeface production programs which allow you to design your own faces, making the supply of possible type absolutely infinite! However, for a newsletter such options will be wasted and, as any busy newsletter editor will tell you, the important part of the newsletter is its content, not the sheer brilliance of its artistic design. But good design is necessary since a poorly laid out newsletter is unlikely to attract any readers. A balance therefore has to be struck.

Since editing newsletters is often the responsibility of just one person, the key to achieving a good layout is to have a standard design into which the copy can literally be dropped with the minimum of fuss and bother. This means that programs such as Ventura, Ready Set Go 3 and NewsWriter are ideal for newsletter production. PageMaker is also excellent for newsletter production but probably needs more experienced hands than the others mentioned, since, as already pointed out, the operator is left to make all of the decisions about such things as where to break an article and to which column it should be reflowed. Ventura, Ready Set Go 3 and Newswriter can make that sort of decision for the operator.

Whatever program you use, it is probably safest and wisest to choose one typeface for headlines and another for the text. These can be mixed in style and in size to achieve variety, but by simplifying matters and limiting your choice you will be able to quickly layout each newsletter. A good choice for newsletters would be Times for the body copy with Helvetica for the headlines. Helvetica is a sanserif face and therefore can produce striking bold headlines, just right for grabbing the attention of the readers. Times is a serif face, and such faces are much easier to read than sanserif faces when a large number of words are printed quite small.

With a column width of 13 pica ems, Times Roman body copy would be acceptable in 10/11pt. If your headlines are across single columns only, then Helvetica should be limited to no more than 36pt. If it is any larger than this you will find words breaking — not a good idea for headlines!

With those basics planned you will be able to go ahead and start producing the copy for your newsletter. This is the next stage of planning. How will you get your copy? Who will write it? How will the copy be submitted — on paper, on disk, by telex? Where will the information come from? Do you need to take out subscriptions to journals, magazines and newspapers? You should consider all of these options before beginning to put your publication together.

If the newsletter is to be a digest then you will need to ensure that you have ready supply of material from which news items and other tit-bits of information may be extracted (beware of copyright — see Chapter 7). If you are going to write original material then produce a list of ideas for topics to be covered, meetings to attend to write about, people to interview etc. Once you are ready to start writing, then use your wordprocessor to produce material before entering it in to your page make–up program. This will enable you to transfer your copy to other programs more easily.

Once your material is written you can lay out your pages according to the design constraints decided upon in your early planning stages. Do not attempt to use too many textual tricks or fancy designs. These will be off–putting to readers. Keep the page simple and straightforward. People who buy newsletters do so for their content, not because they are works of art! Besides, too many design tricks will take up your time which could be usefully employed in writing copy. So, there you have your basic newsletter plan. Define your audience; decide on either original material or a digest; plan your overall layout constraints; keep the layout simple.

When laying out pages in a newsletter it is important to remember that headlines need to clearly relate to the copy beneath them. Do not put headlines above two columns of copy, for example, where only one of the columns is related to the display type. Similarly, do not have two headlines next to each other. People will try to read across from one headline to the next and this will serve to confuse (see Figure 11).

You should also remember the importance of white space. Far too many newsletter producers cram all of the pages with dense type. This is off–putting. White space is a vital psychological element in our ability to quickly read a printed page. The ways to achieve white space in a newsletter include making sure that your paragraphs are short. No paragraph should contain more than two sentences and each sentence should consist of only a dozen or so words. This makes the copy more readable. In 10/11pt Times, for example, these 24 words for a paragraph would take up about four or five lines, about 60pt in depth. Starting a new paragraph after such a depth is important. It means that the last line of each paragraph has a short element of white space, as does the indentation of the following paragraph.

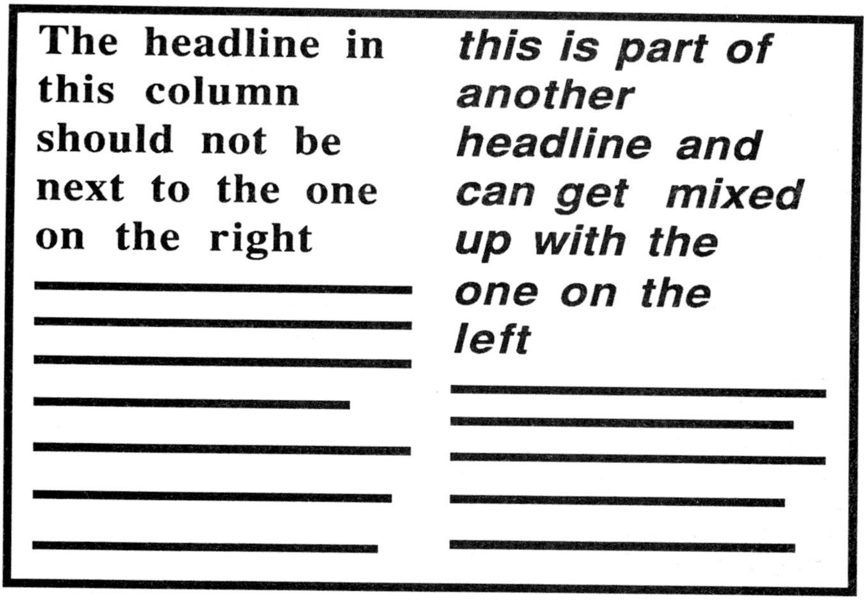

Figure 11 — Headlines should not be positioned next to each other

With these white spaces dotted about over the A4 page, the printed output of the laser printer has a much more pleasing appearance than if there were only a handful of paragraphs on the page. The fact that you are not setting the type solid, but adding 1pt leading is also a means of introducing white space. Another method of introducing white space is to break up your stories with 'crossheads'.

A crosshead is a word or two, usually set one 'size-up', in a space which could take around three lines of text. As might be expected a size-up from 10/11pt is 11/12pt; a size-up from this would be 12/13pt and so on. The word chosen to fill the three line gap in the body copy is usually a word taken from the first sentence of the following paragraph. These are the short, snappy, sub-headings that you see in newspapers. They are used to help break up text and introduce white space to avoid a page looking like a grey slab. As for headlines, avoid them being next to each other in different columns. This will lead to a line of white space across the page, which will make the material look too broken up and disjointed.

Once you have laid out your newsletter attractively you will be able to print it out, then send it off to your printer for producing your run. Don't forget though that this is not the end of the matter. Even before distribution has begun, you will need to start work on the next issue!

Magazines

The production of magazines using desktop publishing technology is not a great deal different to that of producing a newsletter. You need to arrange copy production, distribution and so on, as well as decide an overall design structure for the publication. However, magazine work is a lot more design orientated than newsletters, so you will need to use a variety of textual and layout 'tricks'.

When planning your magazine you should, as for newsletters, decide on a basic layout and produce a grid showing the columns for a page. Many magazines, although they have a basic number of columns, also vary the number of columns throughout the publication. Hence some pages will be designed on a three column grid, whilst others will only have two columns, for example.

Look through a few magazines and you will see the sort of changes which occur throughout such publications. One common factor, though, is that magazines are 'departmentalised' — something which does not usually occur with newsletters. Magazines break up their pages into distinct departments and each department is given its own different basic design. For example, the magazine may have a newsy section designed on a four column grid, whereas the regular features may be on a three column grid, and the special one-off articles appearing on pages with a two column grid.

Before you can hope to put together a magazine using desktop publishing you need to plan the content of your magazine, create departments within that magazine, then define basic layout criteria for each of those distinct sections.

The number of columns you choose for each section will be a matter of personal preference. In general the more columns on a page the more 'newsy' the page will look. Many magazines, therefore, only use three or two column grids (see the Appendix for some basic magazine layout grids). You can make the pages look different though by the careful selection of typefaces.

The body copy of most magazines tends to be in a typeface somewhat more stylish than Times. But you will be limited according to the type of printer you have bought. If your printer can accept downloadable faces, or like the Apple LaserWriter Plus has a large number of resident founts, or can accept founts on plug in cartridges, you will be able to produce good results. Many magazines, for example, use a face called 'Palatino' for their body copy. Others use a typeface known as 'Garamond'. The choice will be largely a personal one but remember that serif faces are the best for body copy since they are easier to read.

Display type for magazines will also be largely a matter of personal choice, combined with the effect you are trying to achieve. Headlines may be in a variety of faces, styles and sizes. It is best to adopt a common type family for each individual section of the proposed magazine. The 'news' section might have display type in Times, whereas the regular features may be in Helvetica, with the one-off articles being in Avant Garde, for example. You should also standardise items, such as picture captions and 'by–lines' (the author's name). Captions, for example, might be in 12pt Avant Garde Italic with the by–lines in 14pt Helvetica Bold Condensed. Whatever you choose, stick to it. Readers like things to be constant. Familiarity is a vital psychological prop, which attracts and retains readership. Don't change your design every week. Keep regular items in the same place in each issue and use the same typefaces for the same functions — captions, bylines, headlines etc.

Once you have settled upon these sorts of items you are ready to put your magazine together. Magazine work is more time consuming than simple newsletters — although these too can be demanding tasks. But magazine readers expect original material. They expect to read about interesting people, and so on. These sorts of items require research; they need digging out. This research can lead up cul–de–sacs as far as writing is concerned, revealing nothing but a dead end. Consequently, magazine writing takes longer. A magazine, therefore, cannot really be produced efficiently by one person.

Indeed, part of the interest for readers of magazines, although they may not realise it, is the variety of writing styles presented. So when planning the production of a magazine it is wise to seek out potential contributors and get them to write regularly.

Newspapers

Producing newspapers on a desktop publishing system is much easier with PageMaker than with any other desktop publishing program. Indeed, PageMaker works so much like a traditional newspaper production office it is hard to see how so many newspapers cope without the benefits of this excellent program.

The only difficulty with desktop publishing systems is that they are largely centred upon A4 paper, unlike most newspapers. There are A3 printers around but these are expensive. Programs like PageMaker will cope with page sizes up to A3, or 'tabloid' as it is referred to. It is in fact not true tabloid, which is both wider and shorter than true A3, but the difference is not too much to quibble over. If you do not have an A3 printer you can either send your disk to a printing bureau, which does have an A3 printer, or send the disk to a typesetter, who can import the PostScript file into a suitable typesetting machine. Alternatively you can print out the page in two halves by 'tiling'. This is a technique used in PageMaker, which allows you to print an A3 page in two A4 halves where, hopefully, you will not be able to see the join! You can design your pages in such a way to avoid obvious joining marks but the best solution is probably to use a bureau service.

Planning a newspaper on a desktop publishing system requires a great deal of skill and knowledge about traditional publishing techniques. Newspaper design is an art in itself and, as any journalist knows, the subs 'bench', desks, where the page layout team sits is generally frequented by people of at least middling years! This is because newspaper design is something which requires a lot of accumulated experience.

Desktop publishers wishing to produce their own newspaper should not be put off. It can be done and very nicely too. Indeed, a number of local and national newspapers in the UK are now using Apple Macintosh computers with PageMaker to help produce their products. The computers can also cope with the production of classified advertising, accounts etc. There are companies who specialise in providing local newspapers with an all inclusive system for the entire production of a newspaper. The capital cost may seem large when you could need 60 terminals say, but is a mere fraction of doing the same thing with a full blown typesetting system.

For most desktop publishing needs though, a full blown system is going to be surplus to requirements. The most likely need for a newspaper from desktop publishing is in the production of an in-house staff newspaper.

Planning such a newspaper requires a bit more effort than a staff newsletter and, as already suggested, does need some good experience of newspaper design. Anyone without experience should consider enrolling on one of the many courses available on such subjects. You should also carefully study daily newspapers for examples of design.

Newspapers contain a lot of information on each page, which is broken up into easily digestable chunks to be read in seconds, or at most a minute or two. These short pieces are then placed on the page in a busy looking design — at least in the case of tabloids — so that readers are attracted. Headlines are short, snappy and contain keywords like 'shock', 'horror', 'row', 'sex' or 'sin', which entice readers to find out more.

Simplicity is still the rule, no matter how complex the page may look. There should only be a few typefaces on each page. Captions, bylines and so on are standardised throughout the publication and regular items are to be found in the same place. Newspaper readers like predictability.

So, when planning a newspaper for the staff, or whoever, follow such tips. Choose a few basic typefaces and standardise anything which is likely to appear in every issue.

Even though newspapers may not look like it, they do have a standard page grid. For a tabloid this is usually around six columns of about 10 pica ems wide. Because of the narrow column width you can reduce the type size and therefore get more words in each column. For a column of 10 pica ems a type size of 9/10pt or even 8/9pt is acceptable and, more importantly, readable.

Newspaper designers use a trick known as 'bastardisation' to make it appear as though the page does not have regular columnar grids. A bastard column is one which is of a different width to those on the basic grid. Newspaper designers often run the text of the first couple of paragraphs across the width of two columns before reverting to single column.

These opening paragraphs are 'bastardised' across two columns and will be on a measure of the two column widths plus the width of the gutter,which would be 21 pica ems for a 10 pica em column. This is not the only trick of bastardisation. A story which appears in four columns can have placed beneath it a story which is bastardised into three columns but running the full width on the page of four columns (see Figure 12). This means that the white space of the gutters between

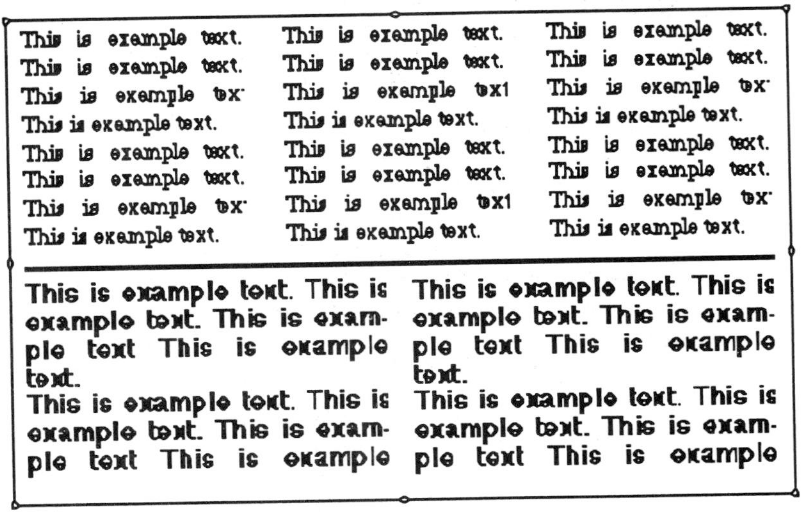

Figure 12 — Bastardisation. The above example shows what happens when a three column grid is bastardised into two columns. It prevents the two white gutters from continuing to the bottom of the page

the four column story run downwards onto text in the three column story. This helps stop the page looking like a page of columns and much more like a busy, readable publication.

Another way of introducing variety into a newspaper page is a 'hanging indent' (see Figure 13). This is where the first line of each paragraph is on the full width of the column but all of the other lines in that paragraph are indented, usually by one pica em. This is known as a 'null on one' (written 0/1) hanging indent — no indent on top of a one pica em indent. Only use hanging indents where the copy will run in a single column. The effect produces extra white space. If this is broken up over a number of columns the effects is lost and too much white space is created.

Shadow boxes are also other design tricks to help make a newspaper page look busy and less like it's made up on a page grid. These are boxes where the right hand edge and the bottom edge have a thick bold line acting as the box's 'shadow'. These only really work over a

> This is an example of a hanging
>   indent. The typeface here is
>   Times Roman, and it is set
>   in 12 point.
> The hanging indent takes the
>   beginning of each paragraph
>   right out to the left hand side
>   of the column, but indents
>   every other line beneath it.
> When a new paragraph is started
>   the line jumps out to the left
>   again.
> The whole process is very useful
>   in page design, but is only
>   really helpful down a single
>   column. As can be imagined
>   this effect would not look
>   right at all if it were carried
>   over a number of different
>   columns.

Figure 13 — A hanging indent. A device used to create more white space on a page. The effects is lost if it is used across columns. It is best reserved for long single columns

single column, and the text inside needs to be set over a measure which is less than that of the column width, to allow for space for the box rules.

A further basis newspaper design trick is a 'WOB'. This means white out of black, a reversal where the words are printed in white over a black background. In fact the words are not printed at all; it is just a black background with spaces where letters would have appeared. Wobs are usually reserved only for headlines. They also should really only use sanserif faces, such as Helvetica, since these have a much clearer definition when printed as a reversal.

Wobs, shadow boxes, hanging indents and bastardisation are the basic tools with which newspaper designers make–up their pages. All are possible with desktop publishing technology. However, when planning a publication, such as a staff newspaper, be sure that you do not use such layout tricks to frequently. One such item of design per page will be enough to make the page look interesting. More than a couple will make the page look too busy. If every story has a different design feature the page will look amateurish. So, like of the other publications we have looked at so far, keep your design plans simple and consistent.

Choose a good serif typeface for your body copy, such as 9/10pt Times Roman. Use Times Bold and Helvetica, for example, for news headlines, with something like Souvenir Demi or Palatino to add a bit of interest and difference to mark the feature pages. In terms of type size, the main headline on a busy A3 size page will need to be around 60 to 72 pt to 'carry' the page. Anything less could get lost in the greyness of the page. Large headlines bring in extra white space to help break up the page.

When writing newspaper headlines remember they are not meant to be literary works in themselves. They only serve to grab the attention of the readers, to entice them into reading the story. They also need to be active rather than passive.

In other words write: 'Gorilla eats dog for breakfast' rather than 'A dog was eaten by a gorilla'. Notice too that you can leave out words in headlines; they do not have to be complete sentences. Also the headline should tell the story as succinctly as possible. It should not try to be clever or refer to some facts embedded way down in the copy. It should really refer to the opening paragraphs.

When dealing with newspaper headlines try to use only a couple of typefaces. The rules mentioned in the section on newsletters about not aligning headlines or crossheads also, naturally enough, apply to newspapers as well.

Once you have planned your basic design considerations you will need to plan a good supply of copy. For this you will obviously require reporters and contributors. If it is a staff newspaper copy could be solicited from heads of departments, for example, or 'correspondents' could be sought and appointed to provide an amount of copy each month. Unless you have a permanent staff of reporters, all of whom have computers, you will receive the copy in one low technology manner. It will be written, though hopefully typed, on paper. All of this copy will have to be re-keyed into the desktop publishing system. You will therefore require a copytypist to perform this work, unless you have sufficient time to do this.

If you already run a newspaper, then it is worth considering the use of machines such as the Apple Macintosh to perform all of the editorial functions. Each reporter can be provided with a terminal, as can the members of the subs bench. A network can be established so that departmental editors can receive copy from writers, then edit it and pass it on to the subs. The subs can layout pages, proof them on a laser printer before sending the pages down the line to the Linotronic typesetting machine. The total investment for a small local newspaper with a half dozen reporters, three editors and four subs would be in the region of only £60,000 ($75,000).

Macintosh software such as Ethos, or Dialtext, are ideal for newspaper production and management. Such systems are becoming more widely used and can handle everything from simple copy to design, newspaper production, advertising, accounts, etc.

In the UK there are some trade union objections to integrated systems, and some printers might not print a newspaper without their trade union colleagues having had some form of involvement in the production of the publication. Increasingly though, non—unionised printing firms are becoming capable of fairly sizeable print runs and some newspaper proprietors may be able to find sufficiently qualified printing craftsmen to take on printing jobs. This is a highly controversial issue though and is one which has resulted in bitter industrial disputes.

The introduction of such advanced technology in the traditional newspaper environment is one which is, therefore, fraught with difficulty. Nevertheless, it should not be dismissed. A network of Apple Macintoshes, for example, is powerful enough to revolutionise the efficiency of the local newspaper industry, and is therefore likely to bring enormous economic benefits.

For in—house staff newspapers companies should avoid trying to take on the task for themselves unless they have sufficient in—house expertise in newspaper design. Whilst a company may employ desktop publishing services in—house for brochures, newsletters and so on, it may be more beneficial to continue producing staff newspapers, or any other kind of newspaper for that matter, using third parties. Costs can be cut though, by using experienced agencies, which employ their own desktop publishing system.

The alternative would be to employ experienced production journalists in—house to take control of desktop publishing. Trying to produce professional looking newspapers without any real training or experience could end up in disaster!

Programs like PageMaker are ideal for newspaper design. If your planned newspaper is to be fairly basic, one possibility would be to have a production journalist, who knows how to use the program, produce the master pages, as well as a style guide. This could then be used by less experience in—house operators to put together the publication. Such a journalist could also create style sheets for something like Ventura, to help with the production of a newspaper.

Brochures

The publication of brochures is an apt task for desktop publishing. Traditional brochure publishing requires the usual time delays of typesetting, and so on. The hundreds of brochures so produced will have to have sufficient information in them to please most readers.

As already pointed out, this is not an easy task and not really desirable. Desktop publishing, therefore, allows you to produce a wide range of brochures for particular readerships. You can even produce a brochure for a specific customer! Planning a brochure is a lot easier than planning a newspaper. There are fewer pages to contend with for a start and design is comparatively simple, although attractive and effective.

Start out your brochure by deciding who it is for and what you want to describe in it. Should it be a sales brochure, or is it a background booklet on the company for new staff? Is it a brochure for the general public, or for technically qualified people? Like any other publication, you must have a clearly defined audience before you put finger to keyboard.

Brochure design is very varied. You may want to publish it in four colour on glossy paper. Alternatively, your brochure may only be a product listing catalogue. Both forms of publishing are available from your desktop system

To publish price lists etc., in brochure format requires an intelligent database package. Something like Omnis 3 Plus, or dBase III is the sort of package you require. This would contain all of the product descriptions, prices and so on. The database could then be printed out with the required founts in the planned format.

This on its own is not really desktop publishing as we have defined it. Of course, the database material can be incorporated into any of the desktop publishing page make–up programs, or you could use a database which stores graphics as well as text, such as Filevision. Alternatively, you could use a new applications generator called 'Clue', which is a database combined with wordprocessing capabilities, and is specifically geared for the desktop publishing of catalogues and simple brochures.

If you want to produce brochures, which are like those produced by advertising agencies using traditional methods, you will need something a bit more powerful. If you plan to produce such brochure, then you will need a suitable program. Something like PageMaker will provide you with a reasonable brochure but if you want display text to be in a circle, for example, you will not be able to do this. You can buy a program called 'Text Effects', which will work with PageMaker to do such textual trickery. But if you are sufficiently knowledgeable, you can program your own textual effect using PostScript, assuming you are using a PostScript compatible printer. JustText for the Macintosh will allow you to do this programming and is, therefore, ideal for a whole range of publications which require more than simple columnar treatment. The PostScript language is in fact quite easy to learn and need not put off serious desktop publishers.

JustText will also allow you to run text around irregularly shaped graphics, a design feature of many brochures and advertisements.

When planning a brochure remember that your text is usually shorter than that which might appear in a newsletter or magazine. Consequently the restriction to serif typefaces can be dispensed with and you could use an interesting sanserif face, such as Avant Garde. This is much more 'arty' and less like a newspaper. It may therefore add impact to your brochure or advertisement. Lists of things, such as names and addresses, or prices, are also often clearer in a sanserif face, such as Helvetica.

Leaflets are also possible with desktop publishing systems. One program for the Apple Macintosh, 'Graphic Works', will allow you to print out a whole leaflet and fold it up, so that all of the pages appear in the right position! The program also has a utility called 'PosterMaker', which allows you to design posters up to a maximum size of 25 square feet! Now you can't print that out on a laser printer, but the program does allow you to print such a poster out in 'tiles'. In this way you can stick all of the pages together and form your poster. However for a 25 feet square poster you would need some 650 sheets of A4. That would take over one and a half hours to print out, assuming it was a very simple design and the printer was working flat out!

Brochure and advertisement, or even poster planning, will require that you have the appropriate program available. This is probably more important than in any other sector of desktop publishing, especially if your needs in terms of brochures are for more complex and more arty publications. Protégé is a program particularly suitable for advertising and brochure production. It is a very capable graphics program combined with a wordprocessor, with business functions, such as accounting, media handling, etc. It is an integral desktop publishing package for advertising agencies, and will allow an agency to design copy, book space, handle accounts and so on.

Office documentation

Every office publishes material daily. Whether it is a memorandum or a report to the board; a proposal for an increased departmental budget or a technical manual, every office publishes something. Indeed it has even been suggested that offices are greater publishers than the publishing industry!

Many companies have been quick to realise that if office documentation is produced using a desktop publishing system the likelihood of it being read is increased! The documentation will, hopefully, look professional, will be laid out attractively and be printed beautifully. With desktop publishing gone are the days of quickly, and noisily, produced dot–matrix proposals. Gone too are the slow daisy–wheel–produced manuals.

However, desktop publishing for office documentation needs as much planning as any other kind of desktop publication. Firstly, as already emphasised, decide on the target audience for the publication and, produce a basic design scheme, even with a layout grid if necessary. If using a program such as Ventura produce style sheets for each type of publication. Proposals, for example, could be laid out in two unequal columns. The narrow left–hand column could contain 'stab points', like mini-headlines introducing each section of the report (see Figure 14). The main body of the copy could appear in the wide right–hand column. Simplicity, though , is the key.

For office documentation two typefaces, one serif, one sanserif, is all that is really required. No tricks like Wobs, shadow boxes and circular text, will be needed. They will only serve to make the office documentation look somewhat muddled and will be out of place in proposals, or manuals, for example. Like all other applications of desktop publishing, you should use the traditionally published material as an example from which to learn. Traditional publishing can do all of the tricks and features with which desktop publishing is able to cope. But traditional publishers have chosen not to do these fancy bits and pieces — they lose readers! Office documentation is fairly sober in most instances; it needs to be. Just because you have

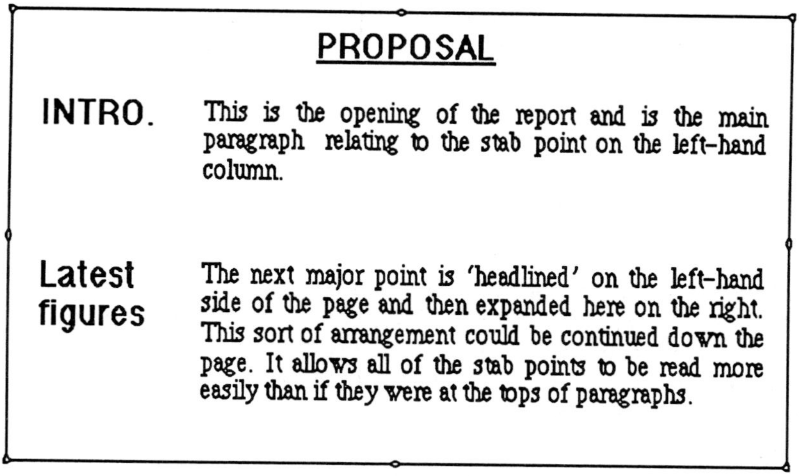

PROPOSAL

INTRO.   This is the opening of the report and is the main paragraph relating to the stab point on the left-hand column.

Latest figures   The next major point is 'headlined' on the left-hand side of the page and then expanded here on the right. This sort of arrangement could be continued down the page. It allows all of the stab points to be read more easily than if they were at the tops of paragraphs.

Figure 14 — Stab points down a left hand column can often make a proposal more attractive, and easier to read.

invested in the latest widget, which makes desktop publications print at 45 degrees, does not mean that your memos have to be printed in this format!

A useful addition to office documentation software is a forms generator. The Rank Xerox system, Documentor, includes such an application, as does Laser Friendly's Office Publisher. FDP, a specialist forms design program is also worth investigating.

You can use these applications to generate forms within the planned style of your office documentation. Again simplicity is the key. Do not clutter up invoices, for example, with boxes for all sorts of product codes and bits and pieces unless, they are vital to your operation. Don't use a box or rule around every single line of an address, either. It clutters the page up with too much blackness and only serves to confuse. Design is also about what you leave out of a page as well as about what you put into it!

It is useful to have a company logo, for example, on all of your office documentation. This serves as the coherent link between all of the different publications you produce, although a consistent range of styles adopting the same type faces etc., is also just as helpful. As was shown for newspapers and magazines, consistency and predictability is one of the keys to attracting readership.

Books

All sorts of books can be produced using desktop publishing. This book is but one example. Desktop publishing can also be used for 'self publishing'. This is where writers produce their own books without ever contacting a publisher. This is a risky game though, and, as always, you must be sure of an audience for the publication. So, just as in newsletters, or any other publication, books must have a well-defined audience.

When planning the look of a book, once again simplicity is the key. Choose a suitable serif typeface and stick to it. Pick the size of the page early on as well. Sadly, book publishers do not work in A4 or A5 or even American Legal. They refer to book sizes as 'Octavo' or 'Quarto'. There are variations on this theme, so that you can have a 'Demi Quarto' page or a 'Royal Octavo' for example. Both Octavo and Quarto book shapes come in four sizes, Crown, Large Crown, Demi, and Royal. Crown Octavo is 7.3 inches by 4.8 inches, a pocket paperback, whereas Royal Quarto is 12.3 inches by 9.3 inches, a colour gift book, for example.

Some desktop publishing programs will not allow you to customise the size of your page, which is necessary for book layout. However, with a program such as JustText you can define your own page size, as you can with MacAuthor. In fact, MacAuthor is an ideal program for book production, since it is foremostly a powerful wordprocessor, but has page make–up capabilities and therefore allows the insertion of graphics, for example. This book was produced using MacAuthor.

Having planned your size and typefaces all you need then do is write the book!! However, one consideration to remember is the pagination. As already mentioned, printing–machines will print a number of pages at one time. Usually the number is a combination of four, eight, 16 or 32.

You should ask your printer what will be the most economical page number for your book. Just going one page over this ideal limit may mean that the printer has to set up a whole new plate with 31 blanks on it. You would be charged for the whole plate, of course, thus meaning that your final page cost 32 times the price of all of the others! Simple economics should be enough to ensure that during the planning of books the most appropriate number of pages is produced. If you feel that the pagination is inadequate than you could lower the type size. However, most books are of single column design. This means that the type size needs to be reasonably large, say 11/12pt, in order to be easily readable. A small typeface over a wide column is difficult to read.

Other Publications

As mentioned in Chapter 1, a whole host of publications are possible using desktop publishing technology. Those detailed so far are only the most common. But desktop publishing systems can be used for all manner of publications such as bus timetables (updates are quicker and cheaper than with typesetting) guides for tourists (which can be updated on a regular and frequent basis) or even individual birthday cards!

All of these publications will need the same sort of planning as any other publishing project. Get a good idea of the target audience, produce a basic page layout grid and decide on a small range of typefaces. Keep it simple.

But this basic page planning and sorting out of the overall look of a publication is not the only preparation you will have to do when involved with any kind of desktop publishing. Apart from such matters as distribution, as already mentioned, there is the difficulty of scheduling, and the organisation of 'copy flow'.

Copy Flow

Copy flow is a term stolen from traditional publishing which basically means the organisation of the day–to–day production of words for publication so that the publishing project can be completed on time. It is no good writing all the copy the day before you need to get the material to the printers since there would be no time to design and make–up the pages.

In traditional publishing houses each publication is gradually built up. No one attempts to start with a pile of blank pages and then fill them up all at once. What happens is a production flow chart is drawn up which allows for more than one issue of the publication to be worked upon at a time (see Figure 15). For example, a weekly publication may contain some news items and some feature articles. The feature articles written in any given week may be placed on pages for the issue two weeks following. This means that when time comes to write the news and deal with the pages assigned to this department, half of the publication is already complete. In this way different aspects of production overlap in any given week, or whatever time period is appropriate for the frequency of publication.

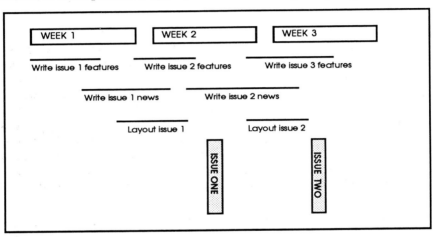

Figure 15 — An example of a copy flow production schedule

An important aspect of arranging copy flow, so that pages may be produced, is the way in which copy will be collected. If you have a network of computers the problem is easily solved since files can be sent to the 'editor' or can be collected by him through the newtork. The copy will be in the right format, easily editable and can therefore be quickly placed upon the page.

For single operators the collection of copy is a little more difficult. If your correspondents use the same computer then all they need do is send you a disk with the files saved in the required manner, depending upon the application you are using, the house style and so on.

Traditional publishers have supplies of 'notes for contributors' outlining how copy should be presented. It is worthwhile for desktop publishers to produce their own such notes, outlining not only how the material should appear on screen but also the application, or applications, which is most suitable, the formats, column widths, typeface, paragraph indentations etc. If contributors are given this information and use it you will be able to place their files into the publication with ease. All that will be required is sub-editing, assuming the material is well written and suitable for publication!

However, many contributors may be using a different computer system, or perhaps just a plain old, low technology electric typewriter. Believe it or not, some writers also still have archaic manual typewriters which require inked ribbons and use something called a carriage return because they are unable to cope with wordwrap! However did they cope in years gone by?

All this really means is that the contributions for a desktop publication will need typing into your computer in the most appropriate format. There are a number of ways out of this situation but all must be incorporated into the copy flow plan. If you have the time, you could type the material into the machine yourself. Alternatively, if you have secretarial help your secretary may be able to do the work. You could employ the services of a 'temp' for a day or two to do the work, or a laser printing bureau, or wordprocessing bureau could take on the task for you. Whichever way you choose be sure to allow enough time for the work to be done and then add a bit for luck!

Another point to consider in desktop publishing copy flow plans is to realise that whilst the technology does speed things up in terms of getting error–free professionally laid out pages out of a printing machine, it can also slow things down. This is especially true in the early stages of desktop publishing.

Firstly, there is the lack of operating knowledge of the programs to contend with and, for some people, there is also the need to understand the whole concept of publishing design. There is quite a steep learning curve for people to adjust to before they are competent at desktop publishing. The second contributor to lengthening the time of page production is what may be loosely called 'creative time wasting'. This is an aspect of desktop publishing which is frequently overlooked. Because the technology lets you to experiment with layouts much more easily and quickly than traditional publishing would allow, there is a temptation to produce a number of different designs for a page before an operator is satisfied. If the operator is technically competent this is nothing more than a waste of time since the first page produced may well have been acceptable to the readership. Getting carried away by the technology should not be allowed to take a hold of an operator. However, for anyone in the early stages of desktop publishing a production flow chart should allow more time than might be necessary in order to allow learning and experimentation to take place. For companies who have been using the traditional publishing techniques of typesetting, production schedules may even need to be slightly extended to allow for this but the hours of waiting for typesetters' proofs which are no longer necessary with desktop publishing, should provide a buffer for the learning needed by operators in the early stages.

Later on, you will find that production schedules can be honed down since experienced operators are able to produce pages of a publication in considerably less time than traditional techniques would have taken. Not only are hours, even days, saved because of the long gone need for typesetting, but sub—editors, for example, can lay out a page much faster. They can see if the copy fits immediately, with no need to wait for proofs, and they can adjust the page accordingly. They do not have to waste time 'casting off' copy (this is the process whereby sub editors count the words in a piece of copy and calculate how many column inches it will fill) and they do not have to spend time working out if a headline will fit over a given measure. In desktop publishing, if it is too long the typesize can be taken down a little, if it is too short words can be added, or the typesize increased. These sorts of operations only take a few seconds but may take minutes of calculation, plus hours of typesetting time, using traditional methods. So, in the hands of experienced operators, it is possible to shorten production schedules, which means for professional publishers that more issues may be produced in a given time period.

Monthlies could become weeklies and weeklies may become dailies. The important thing to remember is that to get the best out of the desktop publishing system you choose, revise the production scheduling and copy flow plan after the operators have become familiarised with the software and are able technicians.

Summary

Whatever type of publication you propose producing with your desktop publishing system you will only get the best out of the machine if you carefully plan your publications. They should be clearly targetted at a specific audience, and should contain copy which is directly relevant to that audience. There should be a carefully considered publication production and copy flow schedule and there should be an overall design concept. This design concept should be as simple as possible, although attractive enough to make readers want to open up the publication and read its contents. The best way to achieve this is to avoid all of the textual tricks built in to many of the page make–up programs available. In other words, avoid using a wide range of typefaces, avoid fancy graphics and designer rules, steer clear of effects such as shadowed and outlined text and do not try to produce something that looks like an explosion in a typesetting factory. You are trying to attract people to read the publication, not convince them to wear sunglasses! Remember, keep it simple.

Chapter 6

Starting Desktop Publishing

Any kind of publishing venture will always begin with the planning and scheduling suggestions already outlined in Chapter 3 and Chapter 5. But the real work only starts to occur when words are put on paper, or, in the case of desktop publishing, on–screen. Consequently desktop publishing projects should begin with the writing of the copy only once the basic publication design has been organised, as well as all the other aspects of publishing, such as marketing, distributing and so on. Some people are tempted to write a headline, decide where the copy will go on the page, then write it to fit the space. If at all possible this should be avoided. It leads to bad writing, since you are constantly worrying about the space constraints, not about the words. Even though this book has emphasised the value of good publication layout, it should never be forgotten that if the words are not right the best layout in the world will not increase your readership. Readers read words and will not go away from your publications, saying, 'Wow, what a great design that page had'. Rather they go away, saying, 'What a dreadful article', or, hopefully, 'I really enjoyed reading that'. It is the copy which people pick up publications to read. They are not students of publication design. Good layout is merely a tool by which publishers encourage readers to look at publications.

So when starting desktop publishing of any kind the important thing to do is to get the words right. Many people, who are using desktop publishing, or who are entering into the world of desktop publishing, are not professional writers. So a few tips on writing would not come amiss.

Writing

As for page design, the real key to writing is simplicity. Any writer is attempting to communicate information to readers. That information is much more easily communicated if it is easily understood by the readers of the piece. There is a wide–range of reading abilities amongst potential and actual readers of publications, and each reader will have a different vocabulary to the next one. It is therefore essential that any publication is written in words which are understood by all. This book, for example, has taken care to explain all of the publishing terminology, since many people new to desktop publishing would not have understood this vocabulary had it been presented unexplained.

In order to make your writing easily and quickly understood it needs to be fairly simple. Your sentences should be short. Whenever possible only make a single point in each sentence. Don't use too many phrases within commas, or half sentences following on from semi–colons. Look at professionally produced publications and notice the length of the sentences.

That last sentence had only 12 words in it, a good length. Try never to have sentences with more than 30 words in them. They become convoluted and, therefore, difficult to follow. An average sentence word count of around 20 to 25 words is just acceptable.

When writing also think about the words you use. For example, don't write 'in the majority of cases' when 'mostly' will do! Don't write 'it is commonly believed that' when 'people think that' will do. Don't write 'on account of the fact that' when 'because' will say the same thing. There are many other examples of such overwriting — avoid them.

Sentence construction is also important. Remember that every sentence must have a verb. That last sentence could have been written as two sentences like this:

'Remember one thing always. A verb
in a sentence.'

However, the second group of words 'a verb in a sentence' is not a sentence in itself, therefore open to misinterpretation. Does it mean that a verb *must* be in a sentence, or does it mean that you should always *remember* the verb in each sentence? For clarity's sake, always construct sentences properly.

If sentences need verbs, one thing they rarely need are adjectives! Don't, for example, write 'this excellent manual is about the very well–designed new widget' when 'this manual is about the new widget' says the same thing.

In general, just give the facts, short and simple. In this way your writing will be more easily understood. Research has shown that readers lose interest as they go through an article. The number of readers which make it through to the end of any piece of written work is far fewer than the number who started. You will lose extra readers if your words cannot be understood. Brevity and clarity are two words which should be at the front of any writers mind. (For those readers who would like that last sentence re–written to make it more digestable sentence, how about: writing should always be short and clear.)

There are plenty of books on writing techniques, which are well worthwhile reading if you are new to the world of publishing. Some are listed in the bibliography at the back of this book. However, anyone involved in publishing should buy the five volume work by Harold Evans, the ex–editor of The Times and The Sunday Times, called *Editing and Design — A Five Volume Manual of English Typography and Layout.* This is an excellent series of manuals for any writer, sub–editor, or layout artist and they should be on the shelf of every desktop publisher, if only for reference. With the knowledge gained from this series of books and, hopefully, the one in your hand, your writing will be easily readable. Prior to publication though, you have to get your words into the system.

Some desktop publishing programs have integral wordprocessors. These are generally not as powerful as full–blown stand alone wordprocessing programs but may be acceptable for simple publications. Since all of the best page make–up programs will accept formatted copy direct from a wide range of wordprocessors, it is probably wiser to write your copy directly into a wordprocessing program. This is a good idea for two basic reasons. Firstly, you can actually perform more functions in most wordprocessing programs than in page make–up programs. A wordprocessor was developed to deal with text, whereas desktop publishing page make–up programs were developed to compile pages, or documents. A wordprocessor is therefore the most appropriate tool to use if you are writing. Secondly, text written into a wordprocessing program is much more easily exportable to other applications, if necessary, than copy produced directly in a page make–up program. You can also have a wordprocessor library of text, which can be used in a wide–range of publications. If the text you require is embedded within a page make–up program it is more difficult to extract it and export it elsewhere.

If you are using a powerful wordprocessor, such as Word Perfect, Microsoft Word, or Wordstar, you will be able to pre–format your copy so that transfer to the page make–up program is simple and quick. You may wish to type your copy into the machine so that it runs across the screen in 12pt Helvetica bold, or whatever your favourite fount is, to make it easier to read. Then, having completed the article, you can reformat and save the whole document, so that it is in 9/10pt

Times Roman across a column width measure of 10 pica ems, for example. When this file is transferred to your page make–up program placing it into the page will be a very fast operation. When using programs like MacWrite, for example, reformat your copy so that it is roughly on the same measure as the columns in your pre-planned page grid. This will give you a rough WYSIWYG of possible problems, such as acres of white space. You can alter these in MacWrite prior to placing the article in the page so that your only real work on the page make–up program is just that — design. Try to get all of your textual work done in the wordprocessor, leaving the desktop publishing software to do what it is best at — laying out pages. When you have written your material, placing into the format it would appear on the printed page helps you to see if the copy is long enough, or too long, as well as sort out any problems of hyphenation and justification, if you are using these options.

Typing copy in 9/10pt directly onto the screen does not help your eyes, since the letters are too small for most screen resolutions to clearly define. Therefore, it is best to write the articles in the format you find easiest to work with, then change to the page format after completing the writing task. The format that you choose for your body copy will, of course, depend upon the look you are trying to achieve. For a newspaper style publication you will need to have fairly narrow columns and the text will need hyphenating and justifying. If your wordprocessor does not allow for hyphenation and justification, do not despair, since most of the page make–up programs will alter the text for you. However, it is better if you can get all of the textual alterations done in your wordprocessor before taking the file into the page make–up program. Although the page make–up programs do have efficient text editors, the whole process of publishing is speeded up if you deal with the text prior to any layout work commencing. This is in fact the way in which traditional publishing deals with the problem of placing text onto a page. Sub–editors correct the material, and cut it down to size, before the material is set for the page. In this way, the problems of recorrecting the written work after setting has taken place, are virtually eliminated.

Desktop publishers will find that they are able to produce quicker results if they deal with all of the textual changes prior to layout, not because the page make–up programs cannot cope with text editing, but rather because when using such a program an operator will want to concentrate on layout. Indeed, a page make–up operator may not have even written the material and will not want to spend some time going through it to check it for accuracy and format, whilst trying to read 9/10pt Times Roman on a small Macintosh screen, for example. Such work is best done on a wordprocessor file by sub–editors.

As already mentioned, text is best printed out in a serif typeface, such as Times, or Palatino, since this is easier to read in quantity and in small sizes. For most pieces of text 'plain' or 'Roman' style will be most appropriate. Italics are difficult to concentrate on if used in large chunks and are best left for captions etc. Bold text is acceptable for short pieces of text but you should remember that bold characters take up more space than plain ones and, therefore, each column will contain fewer characters. This can lead to some difficult word splits in justified text, together with 'rivers' of white space running down a column (see Figure 16). If you do use bold text down a column try setting the text unjustified 'ragged right'. This is the type of format where text does not fill the line width completely and where wordwrap takes whole words down to the next line, if they are too big to fill the available space (see Figure 17). When using ragged right text it is not necessary to hyphenate the copy.

This is justified bold type. It is Times bold and is 14 points high with a leading of 16 points. As can be easily seen there are large areas of white spac which appear to be running down the column as a white river.

Figure 16 — Rivers of white space in a justified column of bold type

There is also a format known as 'ragged left' (see Figure 18). This is where the text is aligned down the right-hand side of the column with variable white spaces on each line down the left-hand side of the column. Most page make-up programs do not use these terms, merely offering menu options for text to be set justified, set left, set right or set centre. For many publications justified text , or set left text will be required. Set right is an unusual requirement, mostly used in magazines and brochures. Set centre is unlikely to be needed for body copy but may be required for headlines.

> This text is set as 12 point Times Roman. It is on an unjustified measure across a single column, and as such is termed ragged right. It is called this because the right hand edge is uneven. The left side of the column is perpendicular, hence only the right is ragged.

Figure 17 — Ragged right text

Using your wordprocessing program to deal with all of the writing and sorting out of the text, will mean that when you come to place the material on the page you can be confident that it is acceptable. If you are using a program such as MacWrite, or early wordprocessors which do not support hyphenation, then you really should invest in a copy of something like Mac-Hy-phen which will hyphenate material for you. Programs like MacAuthor, Word, Word Perfect, Samna 4 etc.,will allow you to hyphenate, usually in a variety of ways. You can either let the program automatically hyphenate the text, splitting the words at points listed as suitable in a 'hyphenation dictionary', or you can manually insert hyphens where you think they would look best.

Hyphenation, though, is more than just a means of making sure that each line is justified without creating too much white space upon it. It needs to be an accurate technique so that it does not destroy

> This text is set as 12 point
> Times Roman. It is on an
> unjustified measure across a
> single column, and as such is
> termed ragged left. It is called
> this because the left hand edge
> is uneven. The right side of the
> column is perpendicular, hence
> only the left is ragged.

Figure 18 — Ragged left text

readability. If you are using manual hyphenation options then be careful how you split up your words. Look at the following hyphenation examples to see how reading problems are introduced if a hyphen is inserted into the wrong position.

per– secution	pe– rsecution
prop– erly	pro– perly
tran– sfer	tra– nsfer

One thing to remember about hyphenation is that it does slow down reading speed. It is therefore to be avoided wherever possible. Hyphenation will creep in to your publications if the columns are too narrow for the typesize you are using. For example, over an 11 pica em column type in 9/10pt is less likely to need hyphenating than type in 11/12pt. The rule is that, for ease of reading, the type size should be reduced as column widths become narrower. Typographers have defined 'optimum' widths for various founts. This optimum width is the widest measure over which a line of text is comfortably readable. As such the optimum width is generally about 40 characters wide. Depending upon type size this will obviously change. For a standard text type of around 10pt this optimum line width is about 15 pica ems.

On an A4 page you can fit three columns of 15 pica ems. This fact explains why for many publications the three column format is so popular. It provides readers with a width of text which is most easily readable, for the type size used. Naturally the column width you decide upon will be controlled by the effect you are trying to create, and the size of the paper but try to remember that columns, which are too wide, become difficult to read unless the type size is increased so that the column becomes the optimum width. Conversely, narrow columns become difficult to read because of the amount of hyphenation and 'back tracking' the readers' eyes have to perform.

Having written the copy, edited and sub—edited the words, as well as formatting it in the most appropriate means for the publication, the wordprocessor file can be saved, ready for placing in a page make—up program. Once all of the copy has been treated in this way the page layout application can be loaded. Some computer buffs may think that having to swap between programs is a trifle frustrating and a needless waste of time when there are applications which will perform wordprocessing *and* page layout. If your publishing needs are simple and infrequent, using such an application may be very useful and economical on time. However, serious desktop publishing will benefit from adopting the technique of traditional publishing of separating the production of words from the layout. Indeed, some publishing operations which involve a number of people would be spoilt if all of the contributors were asked to enter their words into the page make—up program, rather than into a wordprocessor. By punching their glowing prose into the page layout application they would no doubt be tempted to fiddle with design, rather than get on with the important job of writing.

When you have a desktop publishing team the separation of the writers from the page layout software is very important. In traditional publishing circles, writers are rarely allowed to get involved with page layout. There are good reasons for this. Page layout is a skilled task, as is writing. The two therefore maintain a quiet respect for each other.

If you try to combine the two aspects in one by entering text directly into a page make—up application you will end up doing neither writing nor design. The result will be messy.

For good writing results do all of your work in a wordprocessor. Once you have completed the writing task though, the page layout application can be loaded and put to its full use.

Design

With a page grid by your side, and a house style booklet showing all of the rules for the production of publications, you will be ready to design your publication. As mentioned in Chapter 5, there are some basic rules of design and tricks, which will help you liven up your pages. But before you place any articles in your publication, the first job is to produce a flatplan, as mentioned in Chapter 3.

Open up a file in the style sheet format of the publication you want to produce or use the master pages you have saved — the particular method will depend on the type of software you use (for example, Ventura will have style sheets, whereas PageMaker will have master pages), then, with your list of articles, simply write the titles of the articles in the middle of the columns where you want these to appear. You can print this flatplan out as a thumbnails picture with PageMaker. A flatplan such as this is useful. It provides a structure for the publication. If you just fill the publication with articles until you either run out of available space, or you have depleted your stock of written material, the publication will have no structure.

As mentioned in the section on magazines in the last chapter, many publications have clearly defined departments. These are identified on flatplans and, if ignored, will only lead to a random publication. It cannot be emphasised enough that readers like familiarity. They want to be able to turn to page 15 every week and read their 'stars', or turn to the back page of a catalogue every year and find the latest price list. A flatplan may take a few minutes to produce but it will instill a structure for the publication. Avoiding the production of a flatplan like this is likely to lead to the production of a publication, which appears to the readers to be disjointed and without structure, which of course is quite true!

Having produced a flatplan, you will now be in a position to place the articles where they are designated. Most desktop publishing applications will ask you to choose a file from a menu and then point with the mouse to the position where you would like the material to appear. Within seconds the entire article appears on the screen set across the right column width, in the right fount etc. If you are using PageMaker or JetSetter the flow of text will halt as soon as a barrier, such as the bottom of a column is reached.

Ventura users will see their article fill the designated space virtually instantly. Ready Set Go 3 users will find their article flowing from column to column, or even page to page if text linkages have been previously designated.

Production journalists will tend to agree on the fact that one of the major plus points of PageMaker is that once the program hits a barrier it stops, leaving the operator to decide where to allow the text to carry on. This gives you precise control over layout and, although the same result is achievable with other programs, it requires careful planning. However, other programs do have the advantage of automatically dealing with 'widows and orphans' (see Figure 19). A widow is a single word left isolated at the end of a paragraph. This looks unsightly and can be automatically removed by many of the programs available for page make–up. Orphans are like widows, except they are single words, or short lines, isolated at the *tops* of columns.

Desktop publishers should look carefully at the pages they are producing on screen since it is easy to produce both widows and orphans. These textual problems can make a page look unsightly. Fortunately, some page make–up programs automatically get rid of widows and orhpans. However some packages do not do this and so a careful eye must be kept upon any page layout work. A widow could easily be produced if this paragraph were to be transferred to the next column and then suddenly, end with just one word.

The white space above is unsightly and makes the page more difficult to read. Only by getting rid of these problems will layout look professional. You should therefore be aware of these minor problems, and know how to cope with them. The problem above could have been got rid of by lengthening or shortening the body of text in the column on the left. Had this been done it would not have been possible to show you this orphan.

Figure 19 — Widows and orphans

If you are using a program such as PageMaker, which does not automatically dispose of widows and orphans, you should check that they are removed whilst placing your copy. The way to do this is to look at the copy as it is placed in position. If a column has an orphan you can remove it by taking a line from the bottom of the previous column and pasting it in to the top of the offending column.

This will leave a line short in the first column, which can be changed by altering the leading of the text in the first column to add space, so that the extra line is taken up. Widows can be removed by taking lines backwards from the following column or 'running–on'. This means that you delete the 'return' or paragraph marker between each of the two paragraphs affected by the widow. This will remove the offending white space at the bottom of the paragraph and start the following sentence straight away, without leaving a gap.

Gaps should also be deleted if they are obvious between letters. This is particularly true for headlines. When you set copy you can sometimes see small gaps betwen certain letters, for example, between a capital A and a capital V. To remove this unnecessary and unsightly white space the characters need to be moved very slightly nearer to each other. This process is called 'kerning'. It is done automatically in a wide range of desktop publishing programs. You can also perform manual kerning by overriding the automatic feature and positioning characters where you think they look best. This also allows you to perform textual trickery by squashing letters right up against each other — if you ever needed such a design feature which is very unlikely.

The opposite of kerning is called 'letterspacing' which introduces tiny areas of white space between characters which have been set too close together. But this is required less often than kerning.

Once you have deleted all widows and orphans, and dealt with necessary kerning, or allowed your page make–up program to do this, you should check that the article fits the space allotted for it. If it over runs you will need to cut it and, obviously, if it is too short, it will need to be made longer. With NewsWriter the program can automatically make all of the copy fit exactly the required space by altering the leading.

Production journalists will always cut 'from the bottom up'. This is the way in which material is deleted in traditional publishing and is a good idea to adopt in desktop publishing. 'From the bottom up' means just that. The copy is cut line by line from the last line until it fits. Professional writers know that they should never include important facts in the last couple of paragraphs, since a sub–editor may delete them so that the article fits the available space. A writer who includes a 'punchline' as the last few words of an article can see their piece destroyed if the material is cut by the time honoured method — from the bottom up!

For desktop publishers, though, 'from the bottom up' takes on a new significance. Traditional publishing houses do this sort of cutting because it is quick and easy. Desktop publishers are able to edit text much faster than those who use traditional techniques, so why should they cut from the bottom up? The first, and only, practical reason is because it will save you sorting out widows and orphans all over again if your program does not do this. If you cut bits from here and there the article will re–arrange itself and new widows and orphans will appear, making a design revision necessary. The other reason for deciding on a cut from the bottom upwards policy is the fact that the knowledge of this does wonders to concentrate a writer's mind! The result is better written copy and, consequently, a greater likelihood of attracting and holding a readership — the prime aim of any publisher.

Graphics

Few publications consist of only words. Most include some form of graphical or pictorial matter. Indeed, this is the very essence of desktop publishing programs, for unlike basic wordprocessing packages they allow you to incorporate, even draw your own graphical material.

The simplest page make–up programs will allow you to draw your own line graphics, and incorporate shaded boxes, for example. However, the top of the range applications such as PageMaker and Ventura will allow you to place graphics from object orientated drawing programs — such as MacDraw or material from Lotus 123. You can also place material from bit mapped graphics applications. However, these print–out less clearly than object orientated material on a laser printer. Bit mapped programs produce good results with dot–matrix printers but are relatively poor for use with laser printers. If you need regular graphic material to be incorporated into your publications, then it is best to avoid a bit mapped, 'paint' style application if you wish to maintain a good quality output.

The powerful page make–up programs will also accept scanned images from desktop scanners and digitisers. These small machines can scan a page of material on a dot for dot basis and can, therefore, provide an accurate on–screen representation of the image placed in the scanner.

Scanners come in two main varieties, either they are like a photocopier and the material is placed in the machine iteself, or they are based on photo–digitisation where the material is placed in front of a video camera. This technique is likely to be exploited further in the future so that desktop publishers can incorporate images captured on videotape. This is already being used in large newspaper publishing houses and it seems likely that the technology will eventually become available for desktop publishing use.

Using scanners or photo–digitisers is a useful way of incorporating such things as company logos, or complex drawings. The use of a scanner saves time on having to recreate the images on the screen. Once the scanned image is stored in the computer you can manipulate it just like any other on-screen drawing. You can place it anywhere within a document, you can resize it or you can 'crop' it. Cropping is the technique whereby unwanted parts of the image are cut off so that they do not appear in print. Cropping is a technique widely used in publishing when photographic material is to be incorporated into a publication. Some photographs may include, for example, a person who is not relevant to the story to which the photograph is attached. This individual is cut out from the image by cropping. Effectively, the person is masked out of the photograph when the page is made up — the photograph itself is not cut since it may need to be re–used, this time including the previously unwanted area!

Photographs can also be incorporated into desktop publications by the use of scanners. However, the results are disappointing with 300 dpi scanners and 300 dpi printers. In traditional publishing, photographs are 'screened' before printing. In printing it is not possible to show a grey, or a number of different greys, as might be included in a black and white photograph. Instead the photograph is viewed through a 'screen' which breaks up the image into a series of vertical and horizontal lines, effectively creating dots. Where the image is darker, there will be more dots.The screened photograph is called a 'half–tone', since it is made up of either black dots or white spaces and, therefore, contains only two tones. A printer will have a variety of screens available which can break the photograph up into either large dots or small, fine dots. Obviously the smaller screens, the ones with the largest number of lines, produce the best results. Coarse screens can produce dots which are visible to the naked eye.

The type of screen required is often determined by the quality of paper used. If a rough newsprint paper is used a coarser screen can be utilised. However, for smooth, glossy paper a fine screen is needed. Most newspapers will use a screen which breaks an image up into 85 lines per inch, whereas magazines will be using around 120 to 150 lines per inch. Scanners which break an image up into 300 dpi are actually only screening a photograph into a half–tone with around 55–60 lines per inch. This means that the printed dots are visible to the naked eye. For some publications this may be acceptable but until laser printers at 600 dpi or greater become available and scanners improve their facilities to match this increased quality, it is best to 'strip–in' photographic material.

To strip–in a photograph means that you provide the printer with the CRC leaving gaps where the pictures are to be placed. It is a good idea to put a 1 or 2pt box to act as a border to the photograph since this will allow for any minor errors in sizing the photograph to fit the available space. Together with the CRC you provide the printer with the photographs 'marked–up'.

To mark–up a photograph you have to 'size' the picture and record this on an 'overlay '. This is much easier than it may seem at first sight! No photographs are ever going to be the exact size we require them for our publications. Our overall page design and our thumbnail sketches or flatplan will have seen to that! Indeed, when we put together the publication plan we may not even have the photographs available.

So most pictures, or 'pics' as they are referred to by printers, will have to be sized up for reduction or enlargement before they can be placed onto the pages for plate making. This reduction and enlargement is done by a special camera, called a process camera, which contains the screen through which the image is shot. To size a photograph you must first place a piece of tracing paper over the picture as an overlay. Fold over a small portion of this paper and then stick it to the back of the pic. Then with a soft pencil, which will not damage the picture, you should draw lines around the area which you wish to be included in the publication. Then draw a diagonal between the bottom right hand corner of this square and the top left hand corner. Using your 'em rule' — first used when designing your basic page layout — measure across from the bottom right hand corner the required width of the picture as it will appear on the page in pica ems. On the bottom line mark a point where this width ends. Then using the ruler, measure upwards from this point to the diagonal line. This will give you the height of the photograph when it is reduced to fit the relevant width. The height of photographs is measured not in ems, or points but in millimetres! So once your picture is marked up it will have measurements written on the tracing paper cover of so many pica ems by so many millimetres.

If you have a pre–determined size for a picture, which should be the case if you have laid your page out correctly, you will need to adjust the cropping until you get the appropriate size. Professional designers, who work on newspapers and magazines, will often start their page design by cropping a photograph, sizing it up, then laying everything out around it.

However, you need to be a skilled operator at this and will also need to be able to understand and use column bastardisation in order to achieve a pleasing layout. Consequently, this technique is generally reserved for striking photographs, or for pictures where accurate cropping is of vital importance.

For desktop publishers who wish to incorporate photographs into their publications the best method is to mark up photographs, as described here, and then get a printer to strip–in the halftones produced from them when plates are being made up. Desktop publishers should only use scanners if they are using them to reproduce line drawings or material, which is not of the continuous tone type like photographs.

Consequently, scanners may be invaluable for publishers of technical documents and manuals where diagrams, for example, may need to be included in a number of different publications. If these diagrams are already in existence they may be placed in the scanner, read into the computer, then stored for future use. Scanners will also be important for publishers who use material from graphic artists, who do not use a computer. Their material will need to be scanned into the system before it can be used in the publication, unless it is screened by printers.

Many desktop publishers, though, will be using graphics programs, or graphics generators from databases to provide the graphic material for their publications. Each individual page make–up program will accept graphics from a variety of sources. PageMaker, for example, will take MacPaint, MacDraw, Cricket Graph, Full Paint, MacDraft, PostScript, or Macintosh PICT graphics when used on the Apple Macintosh, or Lotus 123, AutoCAD, Windows Paint and Draw, when used on the IBM to name but a few.

Whichever program you use you should check which type of graphics it will accept. If you are about to purchase a desktop publishing package be sure to check which graphics applications it will take material from. If you find that the program will not take material from your current graphics application you may find that you will need a further graphics program and will have to redo any work already stored using the new application. But as more and more modifications are made to desktop publishing packages (upgrades come out fairly regularly) the major graphics applications are catered for by most of the serious software.

When designing graphics material you should, as for layout and writing, remember the key word of publishing — simplicity. Do not attempt to show too much in each graphic. If you want to draw a diagram of how a car works, think about splitting the drawing into a number of elements, such as the electrical system, the engine, the suspension, the interior etc. Each of these elements can then be drawn separately to provide a number of graphics, each of which would be better understood than if the whole lot had been combined into one, complex diagram.

Also, when creating your diagrams try to make them the same size as they shall be when incorporated into the page. Although page make-up programs can crop and resize all kinds of graphics, unless you are careful it is sometimes possible to distort the images slightly. If you can create them in the size you want them this will be time-saving, as well as less likely to cause distortions. However, this may not always be possible as it may be awkward to draw the diagram at the size required.

Another aspect of page make-up graphics is the variety of shades, boxes and rules, which are available within the desktop publishing applications. The shades and rules are meant to be used by desktop publishers to brighten up their layouts. However, most packages contain far too many options, serving only to provide inexperienced operators with a vast array of potentials which, for some unknown reason, get used in every publication these people produce. The result is like something which may be produced by an explosion in a paint factory! When using line graphics, shadows and boxes in any desktop publication the key to their succesful use, is, as always, simplicity. Do not clutter the pages with various shaded boxes, or patterned rules.

To use these graphics options successfully use them sparingly and choose fairly basic ones. In most professionally produced publications you will see only a few basic borders and rules. These are generally a fine $\frac{1}{2}$ pt line (hairline), a 1pt rule, or a 2pt rule. Occasionally thicker rules will be used but these are sparingly applied. A 'thick and thin' rule is also a rule in common use. This has a 1pt line separated by a few points from a 2pt line. These rules are often used to border 'quotes' — material lifted from the copy and placed in a column in something like 18pt type. Quotes (see Figure 20) are used to 'lift' pages of text and are frequently used to break up pages which have no graphics upon them. However, the thick and thin rules, which border such quotes, are, like all rules, used in moderation only. Some publications have a 'column rule'.

This is a fine hairline or 1pt rule, which runs down the middle of the gutter between columns. The most appropriate way of using such column rules is in publications where the text is unjustified. The column rule provides balance to the right hand edge of the columns containing ragged right text. Without these rules the page would appear to have too much white space.

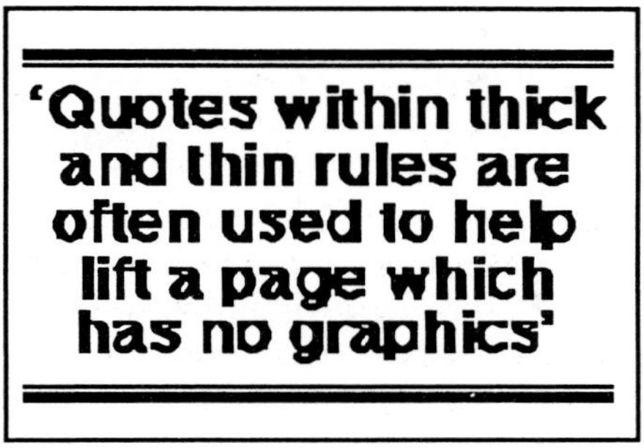

Figure 20 — Quotes within thick and thin rules

One other aspect of rules is in providing a border for the tops and bottoms of pages. Without some marker for the top and bottom of a page the layout will look as though it is 'floating' and some publishers would comment that the text looks as though it could 'disappear off the top of the page'. The way to avoid this rather open look is to place borders at the top and bottom of each page. Page borders also separate the copy from the 'folios'.

A folio is the basic information about each page. This is usually the page number, the title of the publication, and the date of publication. You could also include volume and issue numbers if necessary, as well as small logos, for example. Most of the desktop publishing applications have automatic page number generators, which means that all you need to do is to set up the style and position for this part of the folio in a master page. Folios are useful for readers, since they let them know where they are in a publication. They also provide another use. In these days of photocopying, folios provide a record of where the information is copied from. Such copying, though, may be an infringement of copyright (see Chapter 7).

Generally speaking, folios are in something like 9 or 10pt type and the page border rules are around 2pt, or may be a thick and thin combination rule. You will rarely find complex page borders or striped lines, for example, which are available using some page make–up programs. Such rules and borders are distracting to the eye and will, therefore, only help to lose you readers.

Page make–up programs also offer a variety of shades and patterns with which you can fill boxes. If you look at traditionally published material you will rarely find such examples. The reason is that they are distracting, and off–putting for readers. Shaded boxes are used from time to time. These are generally a tint, which represents a grey of 20 per cent of black — one dot for every five of a black box.

These tints are used as backgrounds for such things as boxed tables, or for lists and so on. You will be hard–pushed to find many publications which have fancy fill patterns available in some desktop publishing programs for such boxes. The reasons are based upon the fact that the key to obtaining and maintaining readership is simplicity of overall design. That does not mean that you cannot be artistic but it means that you must make it easy on the eye of your readers. If your page make–up program has a variety of fill options you will be better off avoiding most of them and just using the 20 per cent tint or nearest equivalent.

The fancy effects should generally be left for use by people with publication design experience. For such operators the use of the various backgrounds and fill patterns can be useful, especially for such items as providing a background pattern for an initial 'drop cap' (see Figure 21). A drop cap is the first letter of an article, sometimes a section of an article, which is set in a typesize considerably larger than the body copy. A drop cap may be 24 pts, for example, whereas the rest of the text is only 10pt. The text next to the drop cap will obviously run over a shorter column width until it

> **T**his is an example of text where a drop cap has been used to introduce the body copy. As can be seen the text on the first few lines is on a narrower column width than the material below the letter, to allow for the extra width of the capital T. The capital letter could have been set on a shaded background for extra effect, or even on a fancy fill pattern, such as horizontal lines.

Figure 21 — A drop cap on a fancy background

reaches the bottom of the letter when it will then run under the large letter to fill the whole column width. JustText, for example, has an automatic method of adjusting column widths to allow for drop caps. Other programs though, need the operator to adjust the columns widths manually to cope with the extra sized letter.

Drop caps are best left for magazine work, and will probably look out of place in company reports, proposals and so on. They should also be used sparingly, although two or three large ones can help to lift a page which contains virtually only text. They break up the page and introduce a small amount of white space, thus livening up the layout.

Small graphics created from the lines and shades available in most desktop publishing applications can also be used as text breakers. These can be inserted instead of crossheads. For example, a 12pt black rule across 10 pica ems in a 15 pica ems column is very effective in breaking up text, providing sufficient white space is left above and below the rule. But like all aspects of page layout, such design effects in page layout should be used sparingly. There is a saying amongst newspaper journalists, which applies to writers as well as page layout artists, 'If in doubt — leave it out'. In other words, when designing your publication only include the material that you know is vital. If you have second thoughts about something, cut it out!

Summary

Hopefully, this chapter will have shown that the key concept of publishing is overall simplicity allowing ease of readership. The copy should be clear and concise, the page attractive but not complicated and any graphics should be simple to understand. By using a wordprocessor for text you will be able to provide better shaped copy; by using draw programs you will be able to provide good graphics.

If you need to use photographs, get these stripped in by printers — at least until technology improves. And if you must use line graphic options use them sparingly. Try to make your layouts attractive, simple and effective. After all, you are not producing a publication which has to use every available design trick in your program. You are attempting to get readers to read and understand the contents of the publication. That is best achieved by presenting them with a publication which looks professional.

The overuse of some aspects of desktop publishing technology will do precisely the opposite, making your pages look like they have been put together by amateurs. The real answer to this problem, apart from employing experienced designers and production journalists, is to study all sorts of traditionally produced publications and base your efforts on them. Desktop publishing is only a tool by which the material is produced.

Chapter 7

Beyond Desktop Publishing

Whatever type of publishing operation you are involved in, getting the material in print is the least of your problems! Whether you are producing a business proposal, or a magazine for half a million people, you still have the problem of getting people interested in reading the publication. Having done that, you have to get the publication to these potential readers. These are problems of marketing and distribution, and are the keys to the success or downfall of a wide-range of publications from simple low circulation free newsletters, to glossy, four colour, magazines sold on newstands.

The only sort of publication, which is unlikely to suffer difficulty, is a very low circulation office-based document, which is only for internal circulation to selected readers; or a similar publication which is for consumption only by selected outsiders. The vast majority of publications, though, require people to have heard of them, to be able to get hold of a copy, then to be interested enough to pick it up and read it.

Marketing

Take, as an example, a newsletter which will be of interest to a fairly small, but distinct, audience, which is widely spread around the country. Say you want to sell the publication to these potential readers. How do you let them know that the publication is available? How do you even know who will make up the potential readership?You could advertise widely on television, radio and throughout the national press. That could bankrupt you and if it only provides a couple of thousand readers it would have been a completely worthless exercise. You could identify key publications which are likely to be read by your potential readers and place advertisements in them. Again this could be expensive. Alternatively you could contact the publishers of such publications and negotiate a deal. You could offer them free advertising space in your publication, in return for free space in their magazine to announce the arrival of your newsletter. Providing the publications are obviously not in competition with each other most publishers would be happy to enter into such an arrangement.

However, simple advertising on its own is rarely enough. Even if your advertisements contain special offers such, as '15 issues for the price of 12', or whatever, you will be unlikely to receive a vast sack of mail demanding copies. You will need to contact people direct, if at all possible, to convince them that they need to subscribe to your newsletter. If you have an identifiable audience, and as already explained this is a necessity, then you may be able to locate an existing mailing list. There are a number of agencies who compile mailing lists of all sorts of groups of people and professional bodies, trade groupings etc., all have their own lists. For a fee you may be allowed access to this list, or provide the owners of the list with your 'direct mail shot' for distribution.

A direct mail shot for a publication is a good method of soliciting readers, especially for newsletters. The mail shot should include a letter introducing the publication and detailing subscription rates, as well as an order form, a sample copy of the publication and a reply paid envelope. The sample copy of the publication is important, since it gives the potential reader a much clearer idea of the newsletter than your covering letter might have been able to do. Without this sample copy people may not be tempted to subscribe and you would lose a potential reader. The reply paid envelope is also important. Many businesses experience the fact that when people do not have to pay for the return postage to any offer they are more likely to apply! A further way of soliciting subscriptions is to supply copies of the publication and order forms at various meetings and conferences, for example, where potential readers may be present.

You should also always include a subscription form in your newsletter. Most publications are read by more than one person, since they are passed around. Indeed, publishers generally believe that between three and four people read each issue of a publication. Consequently, if your newsletter has a circulation of 2,500 you could estimate your readership as high as 10,000. However, be careful of using such estimates, especially if you intend to base advertising rates on them — advertisers will want to see evidence of these claims!

By clipping a subscription form into your newsletter the additional readers, who are looking at another subscriber's copy should be tempted to tear out the form and subscribe themselves! You could also offer incentives for existing subscribers to take out gift subscriptions for their friends, or for just introducing new subscribers. One thing you should not overlook is the power of word of mouth. If you provide a good, readable newsletter, which is informative, and entertaining, your subscribers will tell their friends and colleagues so that they too take out a subscription. Also try to get respected figures as subscribers, so that they can tell people they meet to subscribe. A word or two in support of your newsletter from some leading commentator in the field could do wonders, especially if these people mention the publication at a packed conference!

Distribution

All these tips depend upon the fact that you have been able to get copies of your publication to the readers. For a newsletter with a small circulation the best way is by post. If the circulation really is small it is possible to do this on your own with the help of a suitable database program, which can do label printing. This database could also include information on such things as when subscriptions are due for renewal; which sorts of services individuals have bought, if you have these 'added value' extras in your publications; and lists of potential contributors. In fact, no publication can operate efficiently without a proper database. For large publishing operations something like dBase III or Omnis 3 Plus will be required.

For single operators smaller and less powerful programs may be suitable. The database market is immense and you should choose carefully the sort of program most suited to your needs. Individual writers who use an Apple Macintosh though, should consider a special database and financial management package called 'Writer's Workshop' from Futuresoft in New York. This program enables writers to keep a track of all their publishing efforts, store information on publishers, their rates of pay and so on, as well as offering a bibliographic storage database and a basic book–keeping application. If you have something like Omnis 3 Plus you could produce such a management system for yourself but Writer's Workshop is easy to use and a fraction of the price of larger systems. The details of this book are embedded within one Writer's Workshop database file!

Using your own database management system may be too much work, especially if you are handling newsletters alone. You should be spending your time on writing and editing, without having to worry about organising mailing. There are a number of mailing houses which will distribute newsletters for commercial clients. However, you need to provide these mailing houses with your mailing list — they will not compile that for you! Naturally, mailing organisations will charge for the service but this can be worthwhile, since by taking the work off your hands you will have more time to do the job of putting the publication together.

Mailings, though are not the only way to distribute newsletters. You could make the newsletter available at meetings of organisations where interested people attend, or you could have 'distribution centres'. For example, if you are producing a newsletter on snooker it could be sent in small parcels to all of the snooker clubs where it is sold, say, at the bar. The money is then returned to you by the snooker club, less a proportion for their time taken to arrange the sales. Similar 'bulk drops', as they are called, are possible with all sorts of newsletters.

If you think that you could sell your newsletter through newsagents, then, unless you are incredibly rich or stupid or both, you would be advised to steer clear of this option. Newspaper and magazine distribution, whilst efficient, does cost publishers a lot of money. You will be expected to provide material on a 'sale or return' basis — if the copies are not sold you get them back. You will also be expected to let the wholesalers and retailers keep up to *half* of the cover price for their efforts.

In comparison to the work put in to producing any kind of commercial publication just delivering the copies to a shop, then putting them on a shelf seems a tiny amount of effort and probably does not justify the 'fee' charged. But that is the system which has been in operation for many years and there is no way that desktop publishing will alter it! You may, however, be able to interest a small number of individual newsagents in stocking your newsletter if, for example, it has local relevance, or is of interest to a particular industry, which is local to the newsagent.

But you would have to deliver copies to the newsagents yourself and they would probably only take them on a sale or return basis, wanting a third of the cover price for their 'efforts'. All of these factors have to be taken into account when deciding upon a price, and this could be restrictive, since such an arrangement may make the newsletter too expensive for the potential readers. Altogether, this implies that by far the best method of distributing newsletters is by mail. For large circulation newsletters, the Post Office will arrange collection of the envelopes and can even offer a discount on the total postage price. This is well worth investigating.

Magazines published by desktop publishers may though, need to be sold through the traditional channels of wholesalers and newsagents. However, soliciting subscriptions is of prime importance in the magazine market. Not only do you have a guaranteed supply of readers but they also pay for their copies well in advance of publication.

You can, therefore, bank the money before you need to spend it and earn interest upon it. However, subscriptions also have another value. They allow you to distribute the majority of copies to readers using a postal mailing list, which may be more cost effective than distributing through retail outlets. This helps in keeping the cover price down, and thus may attract more subscribers. So, even if you do decide to sell your publication through newsagents and newstands, do not ignore the benefits of gaining postal subscribers.

The same techniques suggested for newsletter sales can also be used for magazines. But how do you get people interested in your magazine in the first place? And how do you get wholesalers to agree to take on your publication and arrange for its distribution to newsagents? And how do you get all of the various newspaper chains to put copies on their shelves? These areas are very well–organised by the large commercial publishers, who have whole teams of people who arrange these details. Desktop publishing operations are less likely to have such staff, although commercial publishing houses using desktop publishing will not have to worry too much about the distribution problems, which will affect small operations.

However, desktop publishers, who are not part of the established network, have to get a foothold if their publications are to succeed and to be sold through the established network of newsagencies, and newstands. In the UK no publisher can ignore the might of WHSmith and John Menzies. These two companies represent something like 80 per cent of the retail newsagent trade and they also are very large wholesaling operations, which provide publications to many other independent newsagencies. Consequently, a magazine publisher needs to get to know these companies if the publications are to be sold through newsagents. There are other wholesalers but nothing can be as important as obtaining and maintaining a relationship with Smiths and Menzies. In the US, largely because of the size of the country, the situation is more complex with a wide range of wholesalers and distributors.

Large wholesalers will want to ensure that they get good returns from selling the magazines and will therefore push for good discounts.

This will be especially true for magazines, which are likely to have fairly low circulations, although you shouldn't really consider the retail newsagency trade for the sale of publications which are likely to get less than tens of thousands of buyers. The only way to get an introduction to such large companies as Smiths and Menzies is by a direct approach which needs to be thoroughly researched. You need to provide a full proposal document, as well as samples of the publication, together with an outline of the gap in the market it will serve, the estimated level of sales, any regional differences in sales patterns, and an estimate of the amount of money the wholesaler could gross from the sale of the publication. A mere letter asking Mr Smith if he'll sell your magazine will not do!

Even if Mr Smith or Mr Menzies agree to take on the distribution of your publication the battle is still not over. You will have to market it correctly so that people buy it. A shelf full of your unsold publication means that all of the copies will be returned to you as a result of the 'sale or return' nature of the magazine selling business. There will be little you can do with these old issues, except save them in the hope that there will be a rush for back issues.

Another reason to avoid stockpiling of issues on a retailer's shelf is the fact that the retailer will see this happening and decide that the publication is an unsaleable item and may, therefore, decide not to stock any more copies in future. Therefore you must make a major push to obtain readers for the first issue. This will involve advertising, and promotion, in much the same way that advertising and promotion was required for newsletter marketing, although in the case of large circulation magazines a publisher is aiming at larger, probably more diverse, audiences.

Many publishers underestimate the need for advertising expenditure in the 'early days'. The result is that too few people become interested in the publication and, therefore, sales are not high enough. This information is analysed by advertisers, who then decide to withdraw their support from the publication. This leads to no adverts, no readers and no income for the publisher.

The lessons never seem to be learnt, since every year there is a new crop of bright new ideas, which all fall by the wayside as a result of underfinancing for the early days. Because of the relative ease with which desktop publishers can produce material for general sale this sort of problem may become all too familiar. Whilst banks may be prepared to provide loans for capital equipment, they may be rather more cautious in providing cash for advertising expenditure, especially when that expenditure is likely to be far greater than the cost of the desktop publishing equipment! In other words, entering the world of full–scale commercial publishing is fraught with financial dangers, unless you are already rich!

Even if you can afford to get your publication on sale, tell enough people about its existence and attract them into the newsagents to take a look, you still have to get them to pick up a copy and buy it. It is amazing that with all of these prerequisites any magazines sell at all! The key to getting people to pick up your publication is the front cover. Never underestimate the power of the front cover's impact. It can be responsible for the rise or downfall of a particular issue. Many publishers agree on the fact that variability of issue–to–issue sales is largely dependent upon the impact of the cover.

For the commercial magazine market your cover will need to be in four colour, preferably glossy and seemingly with a picture of a member of the Royal Family upon it! The issues of magazines with such cover photographs sell many more copies than others, apparently. Of course, finding an excuse to put a Royal on the front cover of a consumer electronic magazine is a little difficult but the message really is that the cover needs to be striking and eye catching if potential readers are to buy it. Obviously four colour glossy printing is expensive and may well be over the sort of budget many desktop publishers are able to afford. Only the traditional publishing industry is likely to be able to pay out the amounts necessary. The front cover photograph, for example, will cost many hundreds of pounds.

Office Publishing

The largest desktop publishing sector is likely to be that of office publishing, since it will improve communications and increase the professional look of a company — providing the points of this book are taken into account when designing material! The office publishing sector is therefore less likely to suffer the promotional and distributional problems encountered by the commercial sector.

Nevertheless, there are still considerations of marketing and distribution, which should not be neglected. If a company is to produce a staff newsletter, for example, its distribution and the cost of that distribution must be considered. So too must the 'selling' of the newsletter to the staff.

The whole essence of intra-company communication would be lost if the newsletter is delivered upon the desks of the staff without any warning. It could be a case of 'what's this?', then a cursory glance before it is thrown into the waste bin. However, a staff newsletter, which has a reasonable build-up and is awaited with eager anticipation, is more likely to obtain readers, and, therefore, will be more successful in communicating.

Annual reports, too, will need marketing and distributing. Shareholders will expect annual reports but what about all of the other influential people, like bankers, accountants, financial journalists etc., who might like to see your annual report? These people need to be aware of its existence and will also need to be able to get hold of a copy. So it needs marketing and distributing.

There are many other examples in the world of business and industry where desktop publications will still need to be 'sold' and distributed, despite the fact that they are free. All of the design in the world will not help if no-one knows about the publication, or if they do they cannot get hold of a copy. When budgetting for desktop publishing departments, businesses should not ignore the costs of marketing and distributing the products. If they do ignore these vital areas for any kind of publication, then the likely result is fewer readers than required, thus making the whole enterprise more costly than necessary.

Marketing and distribution, therefore, is an important consideration for all kinds of desktop publishing. Remember, computers and their programs are only tools by which publications appear. The problems of design, getting people to know about your publication, then convincing them to read it, apply to all kinds of publication, no matter how they are produced. They should not be neglected.

Legal Problems

Despite the fact that marketing and distribution are major headaches for all publishers, there are other difficulties which should also not be ignored. These are the legal issues of publishing, and, sadly, these seem likely to become more important as desktop publishing multiplies. Many desktop publishers will be unaware of the intricacies of the legal issues of publishing. Large publishing houses have the benefit of lawyers on the staff, who vet material prior to publication. The editor, of course, can still reject the advice of the lawyers but it is a safety net.

Many desktop publishing set-ups, including those in most offices, will be unlikely to have the expert advice of lawyers, who specialise in the main two problems of publishing, libel and copyright.

Libel is one aspect of the law of defamation. It essentially protects individuals from a written attack on their personal or professional reputation. The other aspect of defamation is called slander and offers similar protection to libel, but only applies to the spoken word. (Broadcasting is taken to be the written word, since it is recordable and, therefore, is treated under libel law, rather than slander.) However, the libel law does not try to interefere with the freedom of speech, and so a number of defences are allowed so that publishers can claim that what was published was allowable, even if it was an attack on an individual's reputation. To be libellous the attack has to be unjustified.

There are four main defences to a libel action in the UK. These are called 'Justification', 'Fair Comment', 'Privilege' and 'Unintentional Defamation'. A defence of justification means that the publisher believes it can be proved that what was published is factually correct. If the offending item published contains opinions, or matters which are not established facts, then a defence of fair comment can be claimed. This is where the publisher claims that no malice was intended and that what was written was done in the public interest.

Privilege is the third main kind of defence for libel actions. Privilege applies to the reporting of Parliament, court reports and certain council meetings. Much of what is said in court, for example, can be reported with the protection of privilege, even if the statements published are unfair.

Unintentional defamation is the sort of defence which book publishers may use. For example, a fictitious character may be given an identity, which could be mistaken for that of a real person. The book publishers can claim as a defence that they did not intend to defame the living person. However, no publisher should invent characters without at first extensively checking that they cannot be confused with real people.

To take a libel action against any publisher an individual has to be able to prove that they are the person to whom the article can be reasonably understood to refer; that the material is defamatory; that the material has been published. Publication is taken to mean being read by a third person. Consequently, a letter which is sent to an individual is not libellous, even though it may contain defamatory statements. However, the letter would become libellous if a copy was sent to another person.

Libel actions cannot be undertaken if the person to whom the article referred is dead; if the person defamed agreed to publication of the actual article; if the proceedings are not started within six years of publication; or if an action has already been taken on the article on behalf of the potential plaintiff. Most libel actions are civil proceedings (there is such a thing as criminal libel, but is extremely rare) and take place only in the High Court. This means that legal expenses are very large and whoever ends up paying the legal bills will have to pay out large sums of money. In addition, the jury which sits in the High Court for the action can decide how much money should be paid out in damages if the plaintiff succeeds in the action. Damages vary immensely, but publishers have been forced to pay out sums of £250,000 ($375,000). Costs can also run into hundreds of thousands of pounds. It is therefore no surprise to learn that most libel actions are settled out of court, where the final bill is likely to be much lower.

Anyone who earns their living by dealing with words runs the risk of receiving a writ for libel. Desktop publishers, who do not have the backing of lawyers expert in this field, should be on their guard against libel. The above is only a very brief guide to libel. Desktop publishers really should try to learn a little about the law of libel, to avoid real problems and should establish a relationship with lawyers, who are expert in defamation. Libel is an incredibly complex law and is only ever handled by specialists, most of whom are in London. Names of such lawyers can be obtained from The Law Society.

The other area of real concern to anyone invloved in publishing is copyright. This too is a complex law and needs handling by specialists. Basically, anything that is published has copyright. Publication in this sense does not mean publication to a third party, as it does for libel. Instead it means the first act of putting words to paper — or screen. As soon as something is written, or recorded on electronic media, it has copyright protection. Naturally, for this copyright to be infringed it has to be published to a third party for them to be able to commit the offence!

You cannot copyright ideas, or the basic information from which articles are compiled, except under special circumstances. You can only copyright the form under which the information is presented. Consequently, another author could write a book on desktop publishing without infringing the copyright of this book. But if the new book contained substantial passages, which represented sections of this book, the copyright would have been infringed, even if the bulk of the new book bore no resemblance to this one. The new author does not have to literally copy the entire book to have committed an offence.

In addition to copyright over the actual words used there is also copyright in their typographical arrangement. Desktop publishers must therefore be extremely careful not to copy the arrangement of articles from other publications to their own. This in fact would be a double offence — one for copying the words and the other for copying their typographical arrangement.

Copyright lasts for 50 years after the death of the author of the material, or for 50 years after publication if that occurred after the author's death.

For individuals who write full–time for a publisher the copyright is owned by the publisher, and not the original author, unless contractual agreements say otherwise, and with certain exceptions, such as a series of feature articles which can be turned into a film. For office based publishing, copyright is likely to be treated under the same rules as these, in other words in most instances copyright is owned by the company and not the individual writers.

In the UK there is no requirement to have the © symbol to prove ownership of copyright, although on most major published works it is included. In the US, however the © symbol is a requirement. So if your work is being published in the US be sure that it contains the © symbol for your own protection.

Any work which is protected by copyright may be copied with the permission of the owner of the copyright. This is best achieved in writing, since it confirms the arrangement. If such permission is not sought, then the owner of the copyright can take action against the publisher who has infringed the ownership of copyright. Copyright is both a civil and a criminal offence. The owner of the copyright can seek damages for the infringement, which can be high. A judge can also imprison copyright offenders for up to two months.

Like libel, copyright is a major headache for publishers. So much of the information which is used to compile published material has already been written elsewhere. It is, therefore, of vital importance that copyright problems are understood by desktop publishers. This could be a real problem for those people putting together the news digest kind of newsletters. Since these newsletters, which are an excellent use of desktop publishing, carry material culled from a variety of sources, there is the ever present danger of copyright infringement. Any desktop publisher putting together such publication should be careful to avoid mistakes. Do not copy directly from sources, and use more than one source for the information. You should also be sure to clearly identify the source of the material. If your newsletter comes from a small number of sources then you should arrange copyright clearance from the publishers. Generally, they are only too happy for the publicity, but you must state that what you have compiled is with the 'kind permission of so and so', or some such similar phrase. Do not avoid this. You could end up in prison!

There are a number of other legal problems, which beset publishers from time to time. These include such things as contempt of court, reporting restrictions, obscenity and official secrets infringements. All of these are legal areas, which need dealing with by specialists. Any desktop publisher should ensure that they have a relationship with a lawyer who has a reasonable understanding of these laws, but especially of libel and copyright.

For small desktop publishing operations a good place to find such a lawyer is at a local newspaper. This lawyer may not be on the staff, but will have a grasp of the law as it applies to publishing. If you are in an office publishing set–up, then the company lawyer should be approached to find out if enough is known in–house about the law as it applies to publishing. If not, the company lawyer should be encouraged to find a colleague, who can be brought in for advice as and when needed. With the increase in published items bound to take place as a result of desktop publishing, there is bound to be a rise in the incidence of claims for libel and copyright. The publishers, therefore, need to be armed ready for such problems and only by seeking accurate legal advice will this be possible.

It is, in rare instances, possible to insure against libel. This is very expensive because of the high court costs involved and is likley to be out of reach for most desktop publishers. Consequently, anyone involved in desktop publishing should obtain a basic background knowledge about libel and copyright at the very least, so that the services of lawyers are not needed very often. There are some books mentioned in the bibliography, which provide comprehensive information about the law relating to publishing. They really should be on the bookshelf of every desktop publisher.

One legal point of which every desktop publisher must be aware is the necessity for an 'imprint'.

An imprint is a short piece of text which gives the name and address of the publisher, the name and address of the printer and the publication date. This data is a legal requirement. However, you do not have to make it too prominent. A good idea is to set it in 8pt Helvetica and run it right across the bottom of the back page. Desktop publishers also use typefaces under a licence agreement from the design companies which originated them. This licence requires all publications which use the typefaces to include a note which attributes the ownership of the typefaces. You will see such a note at the beginning of this book. Another semi–legal technicality is that in the UK it is necessary to deposit a copy of each publication with the British Library for publication to have been recorded.

With careful planning and some luck most desktop publishers will be able to escape the severe penalties of breaking the law. Instead for them the main problem will be in dealing with the next issue.

Copy Flow

Having assembled your first publication, checked it is legal, marketed it, distributed it and sold it, you then suddenly realise that it's time to put the next one together!

The flow of copy, and the production of ideas are the two main problems which face most publishers on a day to day basis. If your publications are being produced on a regular basis you will need to produce a schedule for production, as already outlined in Chapter 6. You will see that publication is a continuous process, and not something which ends with the printing of each issue. You must, therefore, have a steady flow of copy, and a bank of ideas for future copy production. Publishing houses which use traditional methods and large ones which already use desktop publishing technology, never ignore the importance of the 'editorial meeting'. These take place at regular intervals, the gap between depending upon the frequency of publication. Daily newspapers, for example, have two such meetings a day.

Editorial meetings are vital for the production of most publications. They allow ideas to be generated and production progress to be monitored. Anyone involved in desktop publishing should take this idea from the world of traditional publishing on board. Even simple office publishing set-ups could benefit from a regular editorial meeting, which looks at possible articles for inclusion and provides stimulation for future ideas for follow-up and hopefully publication.

Summary

The world of desktop publishing is more than about simply being able to use the technology to its best effect. It includes all of the problems which affect publishers, no matter how their product is produced. These problems, such as marketing, promotion, distribution, copy flow, ideas, and the law, should never be overlooked by desktop publishers. Do not get carried away thinking that the technology is the answer to all of your publishing problems. It may only be the beginning!

Chapter 8

Desktop Publishing in Use

As can be seen from all of the previous chapters desktop publishing has a wide–range of possible uses. Commentators on the desktop publishing industry, and both hardware and software dealers seem confident that the largest area for the use of the new technology is in office–based publishing. However, there is a vast potential for the use of desktop publishing technology outside of the production of business reports and proposals.

A major area of use for desktop publishing technology, and one which could well survive longer than many office systems, is that for the traditional typesetting industry. This may seem an odd thing to say, since the whole benefit of desktop publishing is to avoid the need for typesetting! As laser printers become more and more successful in obtaining high resolutions, typesetting itself will become outdated. Indeed, some industry observers have claimed that typesetting will no longer exist after 1990! Consequently, if typesetters are to remain in business, they must look at alternative methods of publication production and desktop publishing is the obvious answer.

The typesetters, who have taken this step and who have already launched into providing desktop publishing facilities, will be able to take business from traditional clients and put material together faster. This will save time, therefore, making their typesetting prices considerably keener than those of their competitors, who continue to use traditonal typesetting methods. The sorts of services which the desktop publishing typesetters could provide would include very basic laser printed output on 300 dpi machines for use as CRC. They could also offer typesetting and design using typesetting machines, which understand a language such as PostScript. Consequently, commercial clients could still receive high quality output from typesetting machines but in a fraction of the time, especially if they were able to provide disk based files for 'running off' in a typesetting machine, rather than having to get the typesetter to re–key the material from hard copy.

The office publishing boom, so—called, is not likely to reduce the amount of business for such typestters. Not everyone will want to buy a full desktop publishing system. Not everyone will wish to add a laser printer to their system but just send off disks for typesetting output. This is one area where the typesetters will also be able to take business from the disgruntled owners of office based desktop publishing systems.

As has already been suggested so far in this book, publication production is not something which a computer program does for you. It is a skill which only comes with learning and experience. Sadly, some offices will fall prey to believing that a desktop publishing system is the answer to all their problems. After some experimentation and the eventual realisation that they are unable to get the results they want, these companies are likely to turn to specialist typesetters, who can offer design and typesetting output. These companies would be likely to write the material to a disk in the required format, then send this for layout etc., to specialist design/typesetting studios. Indeed, this sort of thing is already happening.

A company called 'Inprint' in central London was the first UK—based typesetting/design/printing establishment to take full advantage of the desktop publishing technology. Inprint provides all sorts of publishing and printing services from simple word processing to layout and typesetting. The company even has its own electronic mail service for clients to deliver material for setting. Inprint also offers laser printing, as well as printing from CRC provided either by laser printer or from a typesetting machine. Altogether, a comprehensive service provided with the help of desktop publishing technology. Other companies now offer a similar service, one being Align Design.

Not everyone wants this full range of facilities. For some people all that is required is laser printed output of previously designed pages, or page make up and print—out on a laser printer. Not everyone will want to buy a laser printer, or buy page make—up software. For these people a 'laser bureau' is an ideal method of getting their material into print. This is another possible outlet for the use of desktop publishing technology.

One such bureau is CP&I Computer Services near Camberley in Surrey. This bureau offers a wide range of clients printed output from wordprocessors, databases etc., using an Apple LaserWriter Plus printer. CP&I Computer Services can also offer page make—up, copy typing and so on. Anyone with any kind of printing requirement, who does not wish to buy a laser printer or go to a typesetter, can use firms like CP&I Computer Services to obtain a rapid and pleasing result. Laser bureaux look like being able to replace the simple wordprocessing bureaux which have sprung up in recent years. The facilities the latter offer will seem inadequate in comparison to laser bureaux.

Another major area of use for desktop publishing will be in book writing. This book was produced on an Apple Macintosh system and printed out on an Apple LaserWriter Plus. This meant that the book was able to be published much faster than would have been the case using traditional typesetting techniques and is, therefore, more up to date. This is of particular value to many publishers, who wish to get topical books on to the shelves of bookstores. Another reason for the use of desktop publishing by writers will be in the rapidly growing area of self–publishing. This avoids the need to deal with a publishing house. The writer produces the camera ready artwork and arranges for the printing of the book without any need to become involved with getting publishers to agree on content, format etc.

There is still the major problems of sales, distribution, and warehousing to be considered by self–publishers — have you seen how much shelf space is taken by 4,000 books?! Some self–publishers have been able to cope well and it seems that desktop publishing is likely to be of benefit to self–publishers, who provide high cost, low print run books for an extremely specialist audience. Indeed, as the author of this book I have in preparation another book on medical editing, which will sell to only a few hundred individuals. No publisher is likely to take this sort of book on board but I shall be able to publish it myself and retain all of the profit, rather than a percentage of around ten per cent as a royalty payment. Other authors are likely to be planning similar sorts of enterprise in other subject areas.

But the traditional book industry is not so likely to take desktop publishing on board as yet. There are some very good applications specifically geared to using computers as a front end machine for typesetting. For most books pure typesetting is the only requirement. Text and graphics rarely have to be merged on the same page. Consequently, the flexibility and graphics capabilities of programs like PageMaker would be unnecessary extras for many book publishers.

Journalists however, especially freelance writers, do seem to be a likely user group, who could take advantage of the speed and quality of output provided by desktop publishing systems. For example, in addition to being the author of books, I spend much of my time writing and editing material for commercial clients. I work as a freelance journalist and I provide desktop publishing facilities for companies, who may require magazines, or reports of conferences etc. In the past I would write the copy, submit it to the client for approval, send the copy to a typesetter, layout the pages, get an initial set of page proofs and send these off to the clients, get the pages corrected, check the corrections, then approve the pages for printing! Now the clients who use my services, get a final page proof as the first thing they see! This only takes a few days longer than it would have taken to provide ordinary copy. So, now my clients can get their publications out much faster than by using traditonal methods. They can also end up with a lower bill! Other journalists also offer similar facilities.

The production of sponsored publications for commercial clients and conference reports is not far removed from the world of Public Relations. Desktop Publishing seems likely to be able to provide PR companies with a whole new means of communicating with the world's media. The Press Office of Apricot Computers, for example, laser prints its press releases. Not a major example you might think but, compared to the quality of material released by some companies, it could be seen as a breakthrough!

PR agencies also use desktop publishing technology. One is called PRISM International. This is a firm of consultants with main offices in New York and in the Thames Valley. In the UK, for example, the company produces a newsletter for journalists. The content of the newsletter is new information, which may not have been notified to journalists and which can lead to the publication of stories in the newspapers and magazines to which the newsletter is sent.

Such newspapers may also be utilisers of desktop publishing technology themselves. The Advertiser series of local newspapers in Poole, Dorset, for example, uses a network of Apple Macintosh computers, together with a sophisticated suite of software, to manage editorial work, advertising, the automatic receipt of copy from outside contributors, as well as other facilities such as production management. Newspapers like USA Today, Today and The Independent all utilise facilities of desktop publishing machines such as the Apple Macintosh. The only reason the Macintosh is so widely used is that desktop publishing software was, until the beginning of 1987 only available for this machine, unless you wanted to pay thousands of pounds for software for IBM computers! Now that comparatively cheap IBM page make—up software has become available, there seems little doubt that more and more newspapers, especially local 'papers and 'freesheets', who need to keep costs down, will invest in desktop publishing technology.

There are many other potential users of desktop publishing. As was mentioned in Chapter 1, the impossibilities are far fewer than the possibilities. Estate agents, for example, could produce much more attractive house details. They could even produce individual newsletters outlining a range of houses for each individual prospective purchaser. The use of a good database which can incorporate graphics, such as Filevision, would be ideal for such a job. Bus companies could produce timetables much faster and update them more regularly with the use of desktop publishing technology. Retailers could even produce their own customer leaflets, newsletters and so on.

Without a doubt, the computers, which only a few years ago were brought into popular use to supposedly make us capable of paperless communication, now seem to lie behind what is going to become the biggest increase in paper based communication we have ever seen.

Chapter 9

Desktop Publishing Help

This chapter is but a brief guide to some of the organisations and individuals who can help anyone involved in, or intending to become involved in desktop publishing. This short directory is not exhaustive. For example, in the UK there are over 200 Apple dealerships, all of whom can provide desktop publishing hardware and software. Some are listed here because they have been providing a large amount of desktop publishing advice. For complete accuracy anyone wanting to purchase computers etc., should check their Yellow Pages directories for authorised dealers of the systems they require.

Up to date details about software suppliers can be found in a wide–range of computer publications. Laser bureaux are listed each month in Desktop Publisher, although some of the main bureaux are also listed here.

United Kingdom

Abaton Technology,
2g CADCAM Centre,
Middlesborough,
Cleveland,
TS2 1RJ.
Tel. 0642 225854
Producers of a wide–range of image scanners.

Addison Wesley Ltd.,
Finchampstead Road,
Wokingham,
Berkshire,
RG11 2NZ.
Tel. 0734 794000
*Producers of the TeX desktop publishing program, an ideal
application for those who require to produce technical and
mathematical text. Publishers of manuals on PostScript.*

Aldus UK Ltd.,
Craigcrook Castle,
Craigcrook Road,
Edinburgh,
EH4 3UH.
Tel. 031-336 1727
Suppliers of PageMaker.

Align Design,
London House,
26-40 Kensington High Street,
London,
W8.
Tel. 01-937 8973
Contact: Stephen Fuller, Martin Ward.
*Typesetting and laser printing bureau. Also provides design
services. Data can be accepted via modem.*

Allied Linotype,
Bath Road,
Cheltenham,
Gloucestershire,
GL53 7LR.
Tel. 0242 518288
Contact: Roger Andrews.
*Manufacturers of PostScript compatible typesetting machines,
the Linotronics. Also produce Raster Image Processors.*

Apple Computer UK Ltd.,
Eastman Way,
Hemel Hempstead,
Hertfordshire,
HP2 7HQ.
Tel. 0442 60244
Contact: David Jones.
Providers of the market leading desktop publishing system,
the Apple Macintosh.

Apricot Computers PLC.,
Apricot House,
111 Hagley Road,
Edgbaston,
Birmingham,
B16 8LB.
Tel. 021 456 1234
Producers of the Apricot Desktop Publishing System.

ARS Microsystems Ltd.,
Doman Road,
Camberley,
Surrey,
GU15 3DF.
Tel. 0276 685005
Suppliers of the Neotech video and image scanners for
importing graphics into desktop publishing packages.

Canon (UK) Ltd.,
Canon House,
Manor Road,
Wallington,
Surrey,
SM6 0AJ.
Tel. 01-773 3173
Sells the Canon Personal Publishing package of hardware
and software.

Cardiff Microcomputers,
48 Charles Street,
Cardiff,
Wales.
Tel. 0222 387579
Contact: Bill Cheal.
Computer dealership which also offers laser printing.

CCA Micro Rentals,
Unit 7-8,
Imperial Studios,
Imperial Road,
London,
SW6 2AG.
Tel. 01-731 4310
Contact: Graham Hallett
Computer dealership which has an established reputation for expertise in desktop publishing. Both rents and sells hardware and supplies software. Runs regular desktop publishing seminars with leading speakers.

Chromasonic Business Centre,
238 Muswell Hill Broadway,
London,
N10.
Tel. 01-883 3705
Major Apple dealer with established reputation in desktop publishing.

Cognita Software Ltd.,
42 Ewald Road,
London,
SW6 3ND.
Tel. 01-736 3637
Contact: Friedman Wagner-Dobler.
Producers of the NewsWriter desktop publishing package.

Compass Press,
Cromwell House,
20 Bride Lane,
London,
EC4 8DX.
Tel. 01-353 7400
Contact: Richard Milton.
Publishers of the monthly magazine Desktop Publishing Today.

Computer City,
5 Alsop Arcade,
Liverpool University,
Liverpool.
Tel. 051 709 5959
Major Apple dealership with established reputation in desktop publishing.

Computer Graphics Factory,
1 Elystan Place,
Chelsea,
London,
SW3.
Tel. 01-581 3556
Contact: Jim Stephens.
Typesetting bureau which also offers design services.

Cotswold Press Ltd.,
Stanton Harcourt Road,
Eynsham,
Oxford,
OX8 1JB.
Tel. 0865 880608
Contact: Pierre Macke.
Offers Linotronic typesetting for users of PostScript programs.

CP&I Computer Services,
72 Branksome Hill Road,
College Town,
Camberley,
Surrey,
GU15 4QF.
Tel. 0276 35168
Contact: Mrs Pat Coupland.
Laser bureau offering all services from copy typing and simple laser printing to page make–up and provision of brochures, reports, proposals etc.

Dataproducts Ltd.,
Unit 1,
Heron Industrial Estate,
Spencers Wood,
Reading,
Berkshire,
RG7 1PJ.
Tel. 0734 884777
Producers of laser printers, notably the LZR-2665 printer which handles pages up to A3 size.

Desktop Publishing Systems Ltd.,
40-60 King Georges Avenue,
Millbrook,
Southampton,
Hampshire,
SO1 4JT.
Tel. 0703 789100
Major Apple dealership for desktop publishing.

Desktop Publishing Company Ltd.,
43 Hithermoor Road,
Stanwell Moor,
Staines,
Middlesex,
TW19 6AH.
Tel. 0753 684633
Contact: Henry Budgett.
Publishers of the newsletter, Desktop Publisher, and The WYSIWYG Video Catalogue — a video guide to electronic publishing.

Digital Technology Ltd.,
275a Fleet Road,
Fleet,
Hampshire,
GU13 8BT.
Tel. 0252 624467
Contact: Marc Balhetchet.
Producers of Forms Design Package and other office based publishing software. Also suppliers of wide range of laser printers.

Eldoncray Ltd.,
137 Stewart Road,
Bournemouth,
Hampshire,
BH8 8PA.
Tel. 0202 21505
Contact: Mac Holmes
Computer dealers who can provide desktop publishing support in addition to hardware and software.

Electronic Printing Systems,
Shogun House,
Newgate Lane,
Fareham,
Hampshire,
PO14 1BP.
Tel.0329 221121
Contact: Paul Smith.
Producers of JetSetter desktop publishing software. Also run courses on publication design.

Gestetner Ltd.,
210 Euston Road,
London,
NW1 2DA.
Tel. 01-387 7021
Provides complete desktop publishing systems, based on the Macintosh.

Graham Jones,
14 Loddon Way,
Ash,
Aldershot,
Hampshire
GU12 6NT,
Tel. 0252 333547
Contact: Graham Jones.
The author of this book and a consultant for companies wishing to enter into desktop publishing. Also provides the production of material from writing through to CRC.

Harram Computers,
11 Guildhall Street,
Bury St Edmunds,
Suffolk,
IP33 1PR.
Tel. 0284 705808
Contact: Tony Joseph.
Major Apple dealer with established reputation in desktop publishing.

Hewlett Packard Ltd.,
King Street Lane,
Winnersh,
Wokingham,
Berkshire,
RG11 5AR.
Producers of the leading brands of laser printers.

Heyden and Son,
Spectrum House,
Hillview Gardens,
London,
NW4 2JQ.
Tel. 01-203 5171
Contact: Elliot Kahan
Suppliers of complete desktop publishing systems including software and hardware. Also provides binding systems useful for short run publications printed by laser printers.

Holdens Computer Services,
191 -195 Marsh Lane,
Preston,
Lancashire,
PR1 8NL.
Tel. 0772 561321
Major Apple dealership with established reputation in desktop publishing.

IBM PC User Group,
PO Box 830,
London,
SE1 2BQ.
Tel. 01-232 2277
Contact: Ian Fraser.
User group for IBM owners and users. Has meetings on desktop publishing, as well as a newsletter/magazine for members.

Icon Technology,
9 Jarrom Street,
Leicester,
LE2 7DH.
Tel. 0533 546225
Contact: Mike Glover.
Producers of MacAuthor and suppliers of MacEqn.

Inprint Ltd.,
39 Chiltern Street,
London,
W1M 1HJ.
Tel. 01-935 7140
Contact: Karen Bernays.
Printing and publishing operation specialising in desktop and electronic publishing. Offers all facilities from basic consultancy to design, typesetting, printing, finishing and binding, laser printing etc.

Itek Graphix Ltd.,
Westlink House,
981 Great West Road,
Brentford,
Middlesex,
TW8 9DN.
Tel. 01-568 9297
Suppliers of the Personal Typesetting Workstation Laser Publishing System.

Laser Master UK Ltd.,
Xitan House,
27 Salisbury Road,
Totton,
Southampton,
SO4 3HX.
Tel. 0703 871211
Suppliers of Laser Master laser printers and the Ventura software package.

M. E. Electronics,
5 Hatherley Road,
Reading,
Berkshire.
Tel. 0734 669480
Major Apple dealer with established reputation in desktop publishing.

MacEurope,
9a Lyne Court,
Church Lane,
London,
NW9 8LG.
Tel. 01-200 3981
Contact: Stefan Young.
Distributors of JustText and Laser Tools desktop publishing software package. Also run courses on page make–up.

Macintosh User Group,
55 Linkside Avenue,
Oxford,
OX2 8JE.
Tel. 0865 58027
Contact: John Lewis.
User group for all Macintosh owners/users. Publishes Mac Times six times each year, obtains discounts on hardware etc.

Mandarin Publishing Ltd.,
The Old House,
Church Road,
Kennington,
Ashford,
Kent,
TN24 9DQ.
Tel. 0233 39776
Contact: David Hewson.
Publishes The Wordsmith, the first UK commercial publication brought out using desktop publishing technology. Also offers a consultancy service for people interested in desktop publishing.

McNicol DataCom Ltd.,
Unit 9,
Hazelwood Trading Estate,
Worthing,
Sussex,
BN14 8NP.
Tel. 0903 210646
Typesetting bureau with design services also on offer.

McQueen,
Elliot House,
8-10 Hillside Crescent,
Edinburgh,
EH7 5EA.
Tel. 031 558 3333
Contact: Derek Gray.
Major dealer in desktop publishing hardware and software. Also a printing firm and, therefore, understands publishing.

Mekom Computer Products Ltd.,
Enfield Hall,
Enfield Road,
Edgbaston,
Birmingham,
B15 1QA.
Tel. 021-454 2288
Major laser printer producer. Markets the Kyocera range of laser printers.

MF Graphics Ltd.,
Austin House,
Bridge Street,
Hitchin,
Hertfordshire,
SG5 2DE.
Tel. 0462 37222
Suppliers of Laser Type V, an unusual package that links a front end typesetting system to a Macintosh and LaserWriter to provide low cost proofing for traditional typesetters.

Microsoft,
Excel House,
49 De Montfort Road,
Reading,
Berkshire,
RG1 8LP.
Tel. 0734 500741
Producers of the Windows package which provides the necessary WIMP environment for desktop publishing on IBM PCs, etc.

Microspot,
9 High Street,
Lenham,
Maidstone,
Kent.
Tel. 0622 687771
Major Apple dealer with established reputation in desktop publishing.

Mirrorsoft,
Maxwell House,
74 Worship Street,
London,
EC2A 2EN.
Tel. 01-377 4645
Contact: Pat Bitten.
Producers of the Fleet Street Editor series and Fleet Street Publisher desktop publishing programs. Also sells Graphic Works and Comic Works.

Newcastle Computer Services,
906-908 Shields Road,
Newcastle–upon–Tyne.
Tel. 0632 761168
Major Apple dealer with established reputation in desktop publishing.

P&P Micro Distributors Ltd.,
Todd Hall Road,
Carrs industrial Estate,
Haslingden,
Rossendale,
Lancashire,
BB4 5HU.
Tel. 0706 217744
Major software distributors supplying wide range of programs including the Macintosh integrated package, Ragtime.

Page and Print,
3 Bedford Street,
Covent Garden,
London,
WC2E 9HD.
Tel. 01-831 1904
*Letraset company supplying Ready Set Go 3 software package
for the Apple Macintosh, plus downloadable fonts from the
Letraset range.*

Paintpot Computers,
University Research Centre,
Chilworth Manor,
Chilworth,
Southampton,
Hampshire,
SO9 1XB,
Tel. 0703 760359
Contact: Dr. L. Wardle.
*Producers of FrontPage desktop publishing software for the IBM
XT or IBM AT or compatibles. Also runs evaluation courses for
potential purchasers of desktop publishing software to compare
various options.*

QED Technology Ltd.,
The Priory,
37 London Road,
Cheltenham,
Glouceseter,
GL52 6HA.
Tel. 0242 573344
Contact: Terry Byrne.
*Producers of Protégé and Ethos software packages for use in
newspaper publication and in advertising origination and
handling.*

Quadrant House Bureau Ltd.,
Quadrant House,
Woodman Works,
The Crescent,
London,
SW19 8DR.
Tel. 01-947 7863
Short run printing company able to produce material from CRCs in runs of 25 copies upwards.

Rank Xerox,
Bridge House,
Uxbridge,
Middlesex.
Tel. 0895 51133
Contact: Andrew James, Alan Higson.
Produces the Documentor package of hardware and software for office based publishing. Also owns rights to Ventura.

Scientex Ltd.,
The Red FIRA Building,
Maxwell Road,
Stevenage,
Hertfordshire,
SG1 2EW.
Tel. 0438 351999
Producers of the Protex desktop publishing software package.

Serif Software,
34 Lansdowne Crescent,
Glasgow,
G20 6NJ.
Tel. 041 339 2655
Contact: Mary Sinclair.
Consultancy service for printers and publishers. Also provides software for front end systems, book publishers etc., as well as organising training.

Silica Shop Ltd.,
1-4 The Mews,
Hatherley Road,
Sidcup,
Kent,
DA14 4DX.
Tel. 01-309 1111
Major Atari dealership with established reputation in desktop publishing on the Atari 520ST-M system.

Software Publishing Europe,
87 Jermyn Street,
London,
SW1Y 6JD.
Tel. 01-839 2840
Suppliers of the Harvard Professional Publisher desktop publishing package for the IBM.

Sportscene Publishers,
14 Rathbone Place,
London,
W1P 1DE.
Tel. 01-631 1433
Contact: Roger Munford.
Publish MacUser magazine which has regular information on desktop publishing.

Talbot Computers Ltd.,
293 Charminster Road,
Bournemouth,
Dorset,
BH8 9QW.
Tel. 0202 519282
Contact: Andrew Clunies-Ross.
Provides specialist networks hardware and software for newspaper publishers.

Thames Valley Systems,
Greys House,
7 Greyfriars Road,
Reading,
Berkshire,
RG1 1NU.
Tel. 0734 581829
UK distributors of the MegaScreen for the Apple Macintosh.

The Desktop Publishing Centre,
The Apricot Farm,
57a Hatton Garden,
London,
EC1N 8JD.
Tel. 01-430 0464
Computer dealership specialising in desktop publishing for IBM and Apricot computers. Also runs seminars on desktop publishing.

Typecraft (UK) Ltd.,
Hamilton Road,
Slough,
Berkshire,
SL1 4QY.
Tel. 0753 35156
Producers of the Xtraset typesetting and publishing system for the IBM PC and compatibles.Largely a front end typesetting solution.

Typemaker,
Second City House,
Warwick Road,
Birmingham,
B11 2EW.
Tel. 021-707 8739
Laser printing and Linotronic typesetting bureau. Data receivable via modem.

Unixsys UK Ltd.,
The Genesis Centre,
Garrett Field,
Birchwood,
Warrington,
WA3 7BH.
Tel. 0925 827834
Contact: Steve Downie.
Producers of SoftQuad Publishing software for UNIX systems.
Very good technical publishing program.

Vision Technology,
53-59 High Street,
Croydon,
Surrey,
CR0 1QD.
Tel. 01-760 0013
Suppliers of the Fontasy desktop publishing package.

United States

Aldus,
411 First Avenue South,
Seattle,
Washington,
WA 98104.
Tel. (206) 622-5500
Producers of PageMaker.

Altsys Corporation,
720 Avenue F,
Suite 108,
Plano,
Texas,
TX 754074.
Tel. (214) 424-4888
Producers of Fontographer, a fount designing program.

Apple Computer Inc.,
20525 Mariani Avenue,
Cupertino,
California,
CA 95014,
Producers of the Macintosh and software.

COSMEP,
PO Box 703,
San Fransisco,
CA 94101.
Trade association for small publishers.

Futuresoft System Designs Inc.,
PO Box 132,
New York,
NY 10012-0132.
Tel. (212) 674-5195
Contact: Linda Addison.
Software company providing the management program Writer's Workshop. Also to provide The Publisher Information System an application for small and self–publishers.

G.O Graphics,
18 Ray Avenue,
Burlington,
MA 01803,
Tel. (617) 229-8900
Producers of the IBM package, Deskset a powerful front end system.

Laser Friendly Inc.,
930 Benecia Avenue,
Sunnyvale,
California.
Producers of the IBM packages The Office Publisher and The Office Publisher Plus.

Letraset USA,
40 Eisenhower Drive,
Paramus,
New Jersey,
NJ 075653.
Tel. (201) 845-6100
Suppliers of typefaces.

MacUser Publications Inc.,
25 West 59th Street,
New York,
NY 10018.
Tel. (212) 302-2626
Publishers of MacUser magazine which has regular information on desktop publishing.

Manhattan Graphics,
163 Varick Street,
New York,
NY 10013.
Tel. (212) 924-2778
Producers or Ready Set Go 3.

Meckler Publishing Corporation,
11 Ferr Lane West,
Westport,
CT 06880.
Tel. (203) 226 6967
Contact: Alan Meckler.
Publishers of the Small Press. A magazine for independent publishers, in-house publishers, and desktop publishers.

Mindscape Inc.,
PO Box 1167,
Northbrook,
Illinois,
IL 60065.
Producers of Graphic Works, which combines a paint program with page make–up.

Orange Micro,
1400 North Lakeview Avenue,
Anaheim,
California,
CA 92807.
Tel. (714) 779-2772
Producers of the integrated package, Ragtime.

PCW Communications,
501 Second Street,
San Fransisco,
CA 94107.
Publishers of PC World, MacWorld, and Publish!

PTI Industries,
269 Mount Hermon Road,
Scotts Valley,
California,
CA 95066.
Tel. (408) 438-0946
Producers of the MacVision imaging system.

Seybold Publications Inc.,
428E Baltimore Pike,
PO Box 644,
Media,
Pennsylvania 19063.
Tel. (215) 565-2480
Contact: John Seybold.
Publishes The Seybold Report on Desktop Publishing (a very influential publication) plus The Seybold Report on Publishing Systems and The Seybold Outlook on Professional Computing.

Siemens Communications Systems Inc.,
240 East Palais Road,
Anaheim,
California,
CA 92805.
Tel. (714) 991-9700
Suppliers of laser printers, amongst other electronic technology.

Thunderware Inc.,
21 Orinda Way,
Orinda,
CA 94563.
Tel. (415) 254-6581
Producers of the Thunderscan image scanner for use with the Apple ImageWriter.

Xerox,
100 Clinton Avenue,
Rochester,
New York,
NY 14644.
Tel. (716) 423-4556
Producers of Documentor package, and the Ventura Publisher application.

Bibliography

Designing for Magazines

Jan V White.

R.R. Bowker Company, New York and London, 1982.

An excellent guide to the whole concept of magazine design with plenty of pictorial examples from around the world.

Editing and Design

Harold Evans.

William Heinemann Ltd, London, 1986.

A five volume masterpiece of instructional material on newspaper writing, typography and design. The five volumes are: Newsman's English; Handling Newspaper Text; News Headlines; Picture Editing; and Newspaper Design. These should be on the shelf of every publisher!

Editing for Print

Geoffrey Rogers.

Quarto Publishing Ltd, London, 1986.

A pocket sized guide to editing, typesetting, origination, printing etc., for writers and editors.

Editing Your Newsletter

Mark Beach.

Coast to Coast Books, Portland, Oregon USA, 1982.

Although this book is largely about producing low cost newsletters using 'old technology', it does have plenty of useful tips on newsletter design and production which could be taken on board by desktop publishers.

Essential Law for Journalists

Walter Greenwood and Tom Welsh.

Butterworth and Co., London, 1985.

Largely aimed at provincial newspaper reporters, but contains useful sections on libel and copyright .

Guide to Self Publishing

Harry Mulholland.

Mulholland–Wirral, South Wirral, 1984.

A very useful guide to getting into print on your own.

Hart's Rules for Compositors and Readers

Oxford University Press, 1986.

Widely used in traditional publishing for establishing house styles, and dealing with problems such as awkward spellings, and correct hyphenation.

Laser Write It!

James Cavuoto.

Addison Wesley Publishing Company, Reading, Massachusetts, 1986.

A comprehensive guide to the use of the Apple LaserWriter for desktop publishing.

Marketing for Small Publishers

Keith Smith.

Inter Action Trust, London, 1983.

An excellent guide to the marketing of books for small publishers and self–publishers.

Mastering Business Communication

L.A.Woolcott and W.R.Unwin.

Macmillan Education Ltd., Basingstoke, 1983.

A useful guide to the whole field of business communication, from reports to advertising and graphics etc.

Media Law

Geofrrey Robertson and Andrew G. L. Nicol.

Sage Publications, London and Beverly Hills, 1984.

A very comprehensive guide to the law as it applies to writers and publishers.

The Oxford Dictionary for Writers and Editors

Oxford University Press, 1981.

An excellent pocket dictionary of difficult spellings, unusual abbreviations, etc. Every desktop publisher should have a copy.

Pocket Style Book

The Economist Publications Ltd, London, 1986.

This is the house style book of The Economist *and is a very useful set of rules for any publisher.*

PostScript Language Tutorial and Cookbook

Adobe Systems Incorporated.

Addison Wesley Publishing Company, Reading, Massachusetts, 1985.

An introduction to the PostScript language, together with some useful routines.

PostScript Language Reference Manual

Adobe Systems Incorporated.

Addison Wesley Publishing Company, Reading, Masscahusetts, 1985.

The comprehensive guide and reference text on this page description language.

The Print Production Handbook

David Bann.

Quarto Publishing Ltd, London, 1986.

A pocket sized guide to typesetting, origination, printing, finishing, binding, etc. Very useful for anyone who wants to know more about printing.

The Writer and the Word Processor

Ray Hammond.

Coronet Books, London, 1984.

A comprehensive guide to wordprocessing for all kinds of writers. Not about desktop publishing as such but very useful.

Word Processing for Business Publications

Herman Holtz.

McGraw Hill Book Company, New York, 1985.

A thorough guide to the production of business communications using wordprocessors. Not exactly about desktop publishing, but nevertheless a useful guide to producing office publications.

Glossary

Ad:Ed ratio
The proportion of advertising to editorial space.

Artwork
An original copy of a page which can be used as a basis for printing.

Ascender
That portion of a character which rises above the line of text.

Bleed
The area of the page between the outside edge of the margin and the edge of the page. In most cases this is not printed upon, but for magazine work bleed printing may be necessary.

Blow up
Publishing terminology for enlarging a photograph.

Body copy
The main textual content of a publication.

Bromide
A special sort of coated paper upon which phototypeset material is printed.

Bulk dropping
Delivery of multiple copies of a publication to a small number of places where they can be collected by readers.

Bullet
A large black blob sometimes used to introduce lists or points to make them stand out in body copy.

By-line
The name of the author of an article as printed on the page.

Caps
Upper case letters — capitals.

Caption
The short piece of text which describes a photograph or a graphic on a page.

Case binding
The hard back binding of books.

Casting off
Calculation of the exact length of a piece of copy when set in a particular fount.

Collating
The process whereby printers put the pages of a publication together in the correct order.

Colour separation
The electronic process whereby colour photographs and graphics are separated into the four basic printing colours — black, cyan, yellow and magenta.

Compositor
The skilled member of a typesetting team who actually lays out the bromides in the correct position on a page.

Continuous tone
A photograph in black and white which has continuous shades of grey.

Copy
The written original material which makes up the publication.

CRC
Camera ready copy. See artwork. Laser printer output can be used as camera ready copy.

Cropping

A method of removing areas of graphics and photographs which are not required for printing.

Crosshead

A word or two used to break up long slabs of body copy.

Descenders

Those portions of characters which fall below the line of the text.

Digitiser

A device which converts images such as graphics and photographs into electronic information which can be manipulated by a computer.

Display type

Large sizes of type which are used for headlines, etc.

Dot for dot

A special technique for the reproduction of photographic material which has already been screened.

DPI

Dots per inch. Usually taken to refer to the number of dots in one direction on a laser printer. The actual number of dots per square inch is the information of most significance when attempting to work out the comparative resolutions of laser printers.

Drop cap

A large capital letter which usually introduces an article in the body copy and which takes up a few lines of space.

Edition

All of the copies of an issue.

Em

The shorthand for a pica em. This is a measurement of width on the page and is 12 points wide. Sometimes called a mutton.

En

Half the size of an em. Sometimes called a nut.

Film

A large photographic record of the CRC, used to make a plate for printing.

Finishing

The various processes which turn the output of printing machines into acceptable publications. Includes trimming the paper to the correct size.

Flatplan

A single sheet of paper with miniature representations of each page of a publication, including details of the contents of each page. Especially used to define position of advertisements in commercial publications.

Folio

The basic information contained on each page of a publication, including most importantly the page number but also the title of the publication, the date of publication, etc. In book publishing a folio is a page of typescript as sent to a typesetter.

Fount

The description of a particular typeface, size, and style. A fount might be 12pt Times Roman. Times is not a fount, but a typeface. 12pt Times is a type size. Roman is a type style. Fount is pronounced 'font' and frequently incorrectly spelt that way.

Four colour

Jargon which means printing in colour. Only four colours are necessary to print the vast range of colours we see.

Full out

Setting text, or a headline, to the full width of the column.

Full point

A full stop, sometimes called a period.

Galley

A column of typeset material, not cut or positioned on a page.

Grid

A blank sheet of paper with lines representing the edges of the columns to be used. Helpful for production journalists when designing pages.

GSM

Grams per square meter. A measurement of paper weight.

Gutter

The small gap between columns of type on a page.

Hairline rule

A very narrow rule of half a point thickness.

Half tone

A screened image of a continuous tone.

Hanging indent

Text where the first line of each paragraph extends by one em to the left of all of the other lines in that paragraph.

House style

The basic rules on writing and typography for a publishing house.

Hyphenation

The splitting of words from one line to the next in a column so that excess white space is avoided.

Imposition

The arrangement of the pages on a printing machine.

Imprint

The information on a publication which details the publisher, the printer, and the date of publication. This is generally a legal requirement.

Indent
Movement of text on a line to the right, usually by one pica em.

Issue
A single copy of a publication produced on a particular date.

Job
The printing of an edition.

Justification
The method by which each line in a column is made to measure exactly the same width.

Kerning
The moving of characters closer together to avoid unnecessary white space between letters.

Keyline
A narrow line drawn on CRC to show the position of a photograph which needs adding.

Landscape
An arrangement of layout where the long edge of the paper is at the top.

Layout
A page which has a rough representation of how the typeset page should look after composition.

Leading
Pronounced 'ledding'. A method of introducing small amounts of space between lines of typeset text.

Letterspacing
The introduction of small amounts of space between letters. The opposite of kerning.

Literal
A spelling mistake in typeset copy.

Litho

The most widely used form of printing, which uses electrostatic charges on a metal plate to determine which areas will carry ink and will, therefore, be printed when pressed on paper.

Make up

The act of composition of a page by a compositor. In desktop publishing the act of using a program to design pages.

Masthead

The main title of a publication set on the front.

Measure

The width across which type is to be set.

Octavo

One of the standard sizes of books.

Orphan

A single word left stranded at the top of a column. Many desktop publishing programs avoid these automatically.

Overlay

The piece of tracing paper placed over photographs for cropping and sizing.

Overmatter

The material left over after a page or publication is filled. Some desktop publishing programs can avoid overmatter. With others you can paste it on to a representation of a compositors working board and deal with it separately.

Pagination

The total number of pages in a publication

Pantones

Premixed printing inks in range of colours identified by code numbers.

Pass for press
The act of checking that all of the material is publishable and the giving of permission for a printer to go-ahead with printing.

Perfect binding
The sort of binding used for paperback books and some large magazines.

Period
See full point.

Photo–digitiser
See digitiser.

Phototypesetting
The process whereby copy is turned into high quality output photographed onto bromide. Not necessary for many desktop publications.

Pic
A photograph.

Pica
A 12pt em.

Pieces
The individual written articles for inclusion in a publication

Plate
A perfect impression of CRC from which actual copies of a publication are printed.

Point
A unit of measurement of type height. There are 72pts to the inch for desktop publishing use but slightly more with traditional typesetting.

Portrait
An arrangement of layout where the long edge of the paper is at the side.

Process camera

The large camera which makes half tones and film.

Proof

A photocopy of a set page. Not always necessary for desktop publishers where the first page out of the laserprinter can be CRC.

Put to bed

To finish all the work on one issue of a publication.

Quarto

A standard book size.

Quotes

Quotation marks, or a small piece of text taken out of the body copy and set in display type to break up a page.

Ragged left

Text which has not been justified across a column but which is in a perpendicular line down the right hand side, so that the left–hand edge of the text is irregular.

Ragged right

Text which has not been justified across a column but which is in a perpendicular line down the left hand side, so that the right–hand edge of the text is irregular.

Reverse out

White text on a black background.

RIP

Raster Image Processor. A device which allows desktop publishers direct access to typesetting machines.

River

A line of white space running downwards in a column of text. Caused by poor justification, a lack of hyphenation, or the use of too large a type size for the column width.

Roman
The basic style of type. This text is Roman.

Run
The number of copies a printer is required to produce.

Run around
Text which flows around the shape of a graphic or picture.

Run on
Extra copies required from a printer after the run is complete.

Running on
Starting a paragraph immediately after the previous one with no break.

Saddle stitch
A staple to hold together pages of a magazine, or newspaper.

Sanserif
Type which has only straight edges.

Scanner
A machine similar to a digitiser which can turn images into electronic information for use in desktop publishing programs.

Screen
A device which breaks up continuous tones into a series of black or white dots.

Sections
Groups of pages prepared in advance of the final print deadline.

Separations
Four pieces of film representing each colour, for four colour printing.

Serif
Type which has curls at the edges of characters.

Sheet fed

A type of printer used for small print runs where single sheets at a time are fed through the printing press.

Signature

Groups of pages which are then joined together in binding.

Size up

To increase text by an increment of 1pt.

Sizing

Working out the reduction or enlargement of a graphic or photograph for inclusion on a page.

Solid

Text which has no leading.

Spread

Two pages which can be viewed together on a desktop publishing system. It is important to get the design of spreads correct since they will be viewed simultaneously by readers.

Standfirst

A short piece of text used to introduce articles.

Stories

Individual articles for inclusion in a publication.

Sub-editing

Checking copy for house style, grammar, spelling, accuracy and so on.

Tabloid

A standard newspaper size. In desktop publishing terminology though, this is taken as A3 size.

Thick and thin

A rule which consists of a 1pt rule and a 2pt rule separated by a small amount of white space. Often used to help break up pages with quotes.

Thumbnails
Like a flatplan but can include a basic design for each page.

Type family
All of the styles of a typeface — eg. Roman, Bold, Italic, Outline.

Typeface
An individually designed group of characters — eg. Times, or Helvetica. These are not founts, as some desktop publishing material would have us believe!

Typesetting
A method of turning copy into high quality material made up from typefaces. Most common form of typesetting is phototypesetting.

Typo
A typographical error. Sometimes synonymous with literal.

Wait time
The time during which a print machine is idle.

Web fed
A printing machine which accepts paper from a large roll.

Widow
A single word left as the last line of a paragraph. Avoided automatically by the best desktop publishing software.

WOBS
Reverse outs (White Out of Black —WOB)

X–height
The height of type without its ascenders and descenders.

Appendix

This appendix is a collection of examples of page layout grids for various sorts of publications. The examples are not exhaustive, but merely serve as a guide to the variation possible without the need to go in for a vast range of options, so frequently available amongst desktop publishing software. An example of the sort of grid not to use is also given in this appendix.

Layout for a simple newsletter

Folio

Layout for a simple newsletter

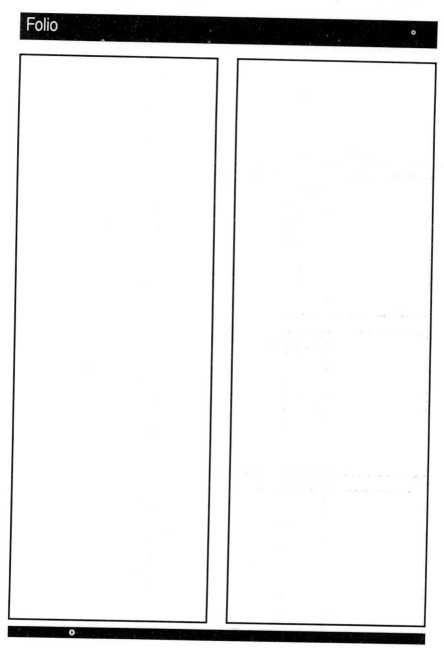

Layout for a newlsetter

HEADLINE IN THIS COLUMN	MAIN TEXT ACROSS THIS FULL COLUMN

	SECOND STORY HERE

	THIRD STORY HERE

Folio

Layout for a newsletter

MAIN STORY HERE

SECOND STORY HERE

THIRD STORY HERE

FOLIO

Layout for a newsletter

HEADLINE 1

HEADLINE 2

Folio

Layout for a newsletter with column rules

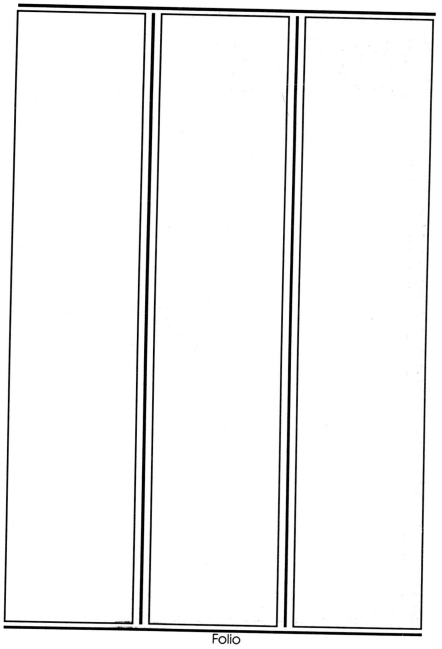

Folio

Layout for a newsletter

FOLIO

HEADLINE 1

STORY 1

HEADLINE 2

STORY 2

Layout for a staff newspaper

Layout for a magazine

HEADLINE

COPY

WHITE
SPACE

FOLIO

Layout for a company proposal

Use this column for stab points	Use this column for body copy

Folio

Layout for a newsletter that will hopefully never appear!

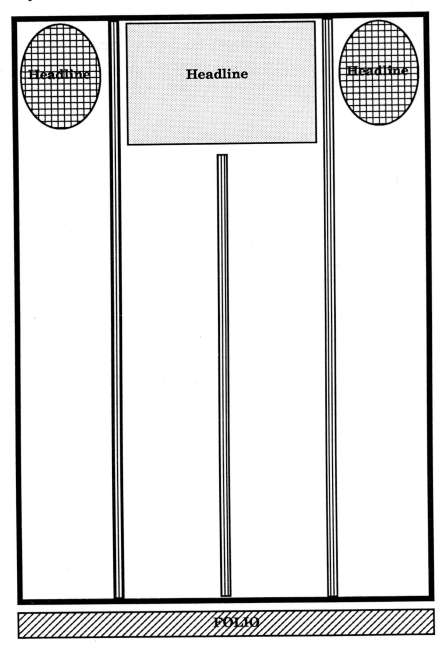

INDEX

Advent 31
Advertising 15,128
Agfa 75
Amstrad 72
Apple 29,62,76,90
Apricot 30,66
Atari 31
Authors 143

Bastardising 91
Binding 48
Books 100,143
Brochures 33,96
Bus timetables 101,145

Camera ready copy 43,48,81,120
Canon 30,69,76
Clue 96
Colour printing 44,67
Column rules 122
Column width 50,83,91
Compositor 11
Contempt 138
Copy 39,101,139
Copyright 136
Costs 18
Cropping 120
Crossheads 87

Data Products 75
dBase III 96,129
DDL 28,74
Design 115
Deskset 73
Desktop Publisher 14
Diablo 75
Digitisers 76,118
Distribution 81,129
Documentor 66,75,99
Drop caps 124

Ems 49
Epson 75
Estate agents 145

Film 43
Finishing 47
Flatpan 36
Fleet Street Publisher 31,70,71
Fleet Street Editor 70

Folios 123
Forms Design Package 68,99
Founts 52
Freelance journalists 13,143
Front Page 73

Graphic Works 73
Graphics 118
Grids 84

Half tones 120
Hanging indent 92
Hard disk 24
Harvard Professional Publisher 73
Headlines 86,91,94
Health problems 77
House style 41,49
HP Vectra 69
Hyphenation 59,112,113

IBM PC 22,29,57
Icons 25
Ideas 33
Imposition 45
Imprint 138
JetSetter 69
JustText 60,100
Justification 59

Kerning 117
Kyocera 75

Laser bureaux 142
Laser printers 17,27,42,74
LaserWriter 75,89
LaserJet 74
Leading 50
Legal problems 134
Letterspacing 117
Libel 135
Line graphics 122
Literals 42
Litho 43
Local newspapers 90,144
Lotus 123 63,121

Mac-Hy-phen 112
MacAuthor 73,100,112
MacDraw 63,121
Macintosh 29,62,76,90

MacWrite 63,112
Magazines 88
Marketing 14,127
Microsoft Word 63,109
Mouse 24

Newsletters 34,79,82
Newspapers 90,144
NewsWriter 59,85,117

Office publishing 98,133
Office Publisher 67,99
Offset lithography 43
Omnis 3 Plus 96,129
Optimum width 113
Orphans 116

Page borders 123
Page description languages 27
PageMaker (Main section) 62
Paper 46
Photographs 119,120
Points 49
PostScript 28,61,74
Printing 42
Production schedule 35,102
Proofs 41
Protégé 97
Protex 70
Public Relations 144

Ragtime 72
RAM 12,23
ReadySetGo3 71,85,115

Scanners 76,118,121
Scheduling 34,35
Screen resolution 12,22
Sponsored publications 144
Sub-editing 40
Subscriptions 129

TeX 73
Text Effects 97
Thunderscan 76
Tourist guides 101
Type 49
Typefaces 51
Typesetters 11,141

Ventura 64,85

Wang 62
Web Offset printing 43
Widows 116
WIMP 25,74
Word Perfect 63,109
Wordsmith 13

Wordstar 63,109
Writer's Workshop 129
Writing 107
WYSIWYG 21,58,84

Xenix 60
Xerox 30,64
Xtraset 73

Other books of interest

Mastering VIEW, ViewSheet and ViewFile/ *C. Williamson*

A comprehensive guide to wordprocessing, spreadsheets and graphics on the BBC computer.

Communicating with Microcomputers/ *I. Cullimore*

All you need to know about how to transfer data between computers – or from a computer to almost anything else!

Mastering the Amstrad PCW 8256/8512/ *J. Hughes*

A simplified and clear guide to Locoscript word processing, CP/M and much more on this popular range of computers.

Exploiting MS-DOS, on the Amstrad PC1512 and all IBM compatibles/ *N. Backhurst & P. Davies*

Suitable for both beginners and experienced users who need to cut the hassle of using MS-DOS and PC-DOS.

The PC Compendium/ Vol.I/ *C. Naylor*

Hints and tips, ideas and opinions on how to get the best from your IBM PC or compatible. Covers everything from mains interference to expert systems.

Computer Aided Design on the IBM PC and Compatibles/ *H. Atherton* (available late '87)

A companion to the Desktop Publishing Companion! If you have specialist graphics needs – this is for you. Shows how to use your PC to produce professional CAD on a realistic budget.

Cost Effective Local Area Networks/ *S. Bridges*

Shows the various ways to interconnect micros to share expensive resources, using commercially available software and the minimum of extra hardware.

Order these books from your regular bookseller, or contact Sigma Press in case of difficulty. We have a catalogue of over 100 books – ask for your copy today.

Sigma Press, 98a Water Lane, Wilmslow, Cheshire SK9 5BB. Phone: 0625-531035